THERE IS SOMETHING NEW UNDER THE RISING SUN ... DID YOU KNOW THAT ...

- *Japan's changing relationship with the U.S. has yielded new Japanese attitudes—such as assertiveness—uncommon only a few years ago?*
- *More than 300,000 Americans are employed by Japanese companies in the U.S.? Are you aware of the character traits most admired by your Japanese boss?*
- *Many younger Japanese couples entertain together?*
- *Japanese corporate and personal relationships are in flux as more and more Japanese switch jobs and make mid-life career changes?*
- *Lawyers, once scorned by Japanese companies, are now being consulted by them? Do you know when it is acceptable to bring lawyers to negotiations?*

Let DIANA ROWLAND be your guide to successful negotiation and socializing in Japan. An American with over twenty years of experience working with the Japanese, Ms. Rowland lived in Japan for six years and subsequently worked as the assistant to the president of a Japanese trading company at its California branch. She speaks fluent Japanese and knows firsthand the ways of the Japanese—and the pleasures and pitfalls of negotiating in a culture so very different from our own.

Currently, from her office in San Diego, California, Diana Rowland provides training and consultation for American and Japanese corporations on effective cross-cultural business dealings.

Please turn the page for praise
from the press and
top businesspeople alike.

"JAPANESE BUSINESS ETIQUETTE is an indispensable guide for anyone who is serious about succeeding with the Japanese. It is a perfect road map for business people from executive to engineer as well as for students, travelers or anyone else interested in understanding the Japanese."
—Iwao Tomita, senior executive partner, Deloitte Touche, Tohmatsu, Japan

****

"A must for Americans who have, or hope to have, any business dealings with the Japanese. Carries the American corporate traveler beyond the Japanese office ... making this the perfect paperback to buy and read now, and take along to Japan someday."
—*Washington Business Journal*

****

"Superb! The best succinct guide to business success with the Japanese. I have ordered hundreds for our Doing Business with Japan program over the years. Good to see that the new, expanded edition is out!"
—Jack G. Lewis, director, IBEAR Executive Programs, University of Southern California

****

"Provides a wealth of information of interest to business people."
—*Publishers Weekly*

JAPANESE BUSINESS ETIQUETTE

A Practical Guide to Success with the Japanese

Diana Rowland

**Updated and Revised
Second Edition**

WARNER BOOKS

A Time Warner Company

Copyright © 1985, 1993 by Diana Rowland
All rights reserved.

Warner Books, Inc., 1271 Avenue of the Americas, New York, NY 10020

W A Time Warner Company

Printed in the United States of America

First Printing: March 1993

10 9 8 7 6 5 4 3 2 1

Cover design by Michèle Brinson
Book design by H. Roberts

Library of Congress Cataloging-in-Publication Data

Rowland, Diana.
    Japanese business etiquette / Diana Rowland.—Updated and rev.,
2nd ed.
        p.   cm.
    Includes bibliographical references and index.
    ISBN 0-446-39518-8
    1. Business etiquette—Japan.   2. Japan—Social life and
customs—1945—   3. Corporate culture—Japan.   4. Negotiation in
business—Japan.   I. Title.
HF5387.R68   1993
395'.52'0952—dc20   92-29483
                                                               CIP

To Mr. Seigo Tabata, whose generosity and expertise at blending the best of East and West were a constant source of inspiration, and to my parents, who taught me to accept and value people as they are.

Contents

Introduction

Since *Japanese Business Etiquette* was first published in 1985, major changes have taken place in the relationship between Japan and America. Corporations in each country now deal with each other across cultural borders with far greater frequency and interact with each other at many different levels. Gone are the days when a business relationship between a Japanese and an American company was limited to a relationship between two CEOs who barely spoke each other's language. Nowadays, Japanese and American engineers, investors, distributors, entrepreneurs, and corporate staff at every level work together toward shared goals. Our two cultures remain vastly different in innumerable ways, yet we are deepening our business relationships more than any two countries in the world.

At the time that I wrote the first edition of this book, few U.S. firms were focusing their efforts on penetrating what had already become the second largest consumer market in the world; they certainly should have been, but they were not. American firms now pursue the Japanese market as a primary requisite for remaining internationally competitive, rather than merely dabbling in it as an adjunct to their activities in Europe and other markets in the West. No longer is corporate America passive in its attempt to penetrate Japanese markets, court Japanese investors, and plug into Japanese research and development. Such imperatives are now considered crucial to corporate survival.

Our two countries have been entwined in a political relationship for decades, yet today our economic and commercial marriage has become one of the defining issues of our time. People at all levels of each society now deal with counterparts in the other. We are communicating face to face, working on the same shop floor, and negotiating partnerships with the Japanese on an everyday basis. Hundreds of thousands of Americans work for Japanese-owned companies both in Japan and in the States, while the number of strategic alliances between firms in each country has ballooned. Americans, however, are still not as effective as they could be—or should be— in interacting with and influencing their Japanese counterparts. Many of our business failings in Japan, as illustrated by our persistent and massive trade imbalance, can be traced directly to our lack of competency and skills in the interpersonal realm, where a minor misunderstanding can often lead to a major chasm.

This book is about understanding the Japanese from the inside out: their values, their business culture, and their unique rules of etiquette and protocol that still remain in place even though the Japanese have become adept at doing business internationally, especially with the industrialized West. Many anthropologists and sociologists have addressed Japanese values and how they affect Japanese culture, but their research is often too academic for the average business person. *Japanese Business Etiquette* addresses how the basic forms of Japanese culture influence business and are vital to business success with the Japanese. Seven years of leading seminars on Japanese business have allowed me to constantly improve and update my material. This new edition, which reflects those seven years of training experience, includes new information as well as fresh anecdotes that illustrate complex concepts.

What's New in This Edition?

In the 1980s, Japanese investors acquired a considerable amount of property in the United States. Opportunities for hosting Japanese guests have also increased. This edition provides the reader with what constitutes respectful behavior: where to take your guests, appropriate seating arrangements for formal and informal times, and guidelines to follow when receiving guests in the office.

Interaction with the Japanese is no longer confined to their turf.

Japanese factories have become the main centers of industry in many small American towns and are supporting local economies. More than 300,000 Americans are employed by Japanese companies in the United States. These people rely directly on the Japanese for their livelihood, and they need to know how to most effectively work with their bosses and fellow employees, as well as how to avoid frustration arising from conflicting expectations. This edition describes these issues in depth, offers a list of character traits most valued in Japanese companies, and describes what one should expect from evaluations.

With economic success has come a change in Japan's relationship with the United States. Numerous books and newspaper articles have observed that the Japanese are displaying a new assertiveness. As they become more accustomed to speaking frankly, many are even criticizing American companies and their practices, behavior that was uncommon only a few years ago. How do we deal with this change? This book tries to lead the way.

In the past few years, Japanese companies have changed their attitude toward consulting attorneys during negotiations. In what was once considered a negative approach, a great number of attorneys are being retained by Japanese multinationals. Western business people should be able to identify under what circumstances it is acceptable to bring lawyers to negotiations and how the use of legal documents to enforce agreements and contracts is changing. New material in this edition sheds light on Japan's changing legal atmosphere and the role of lawyers.

While older Japanese still wield the greatest power in most companies, a younger generation led by baby boomers (some of whom are women) are beginning to command more authority. Western business people must clearly understand the differences between the generations and the implications of doing business with them. Attitudes toward work, the family, and leisure vary widely from person to person, and greatly from generation to generation. Rather than men spending an evening "out with the boys," younger Japanese now commonly entertain as couples. Work attitudes are also radically different; more people than ever before are engaging in job switching and mid-life career changes, which affect both corporate and personal relationships. The many "returnees" to Japan from overseas appointments are beginning to exert new influence.

This new edition also includes a more detailed negotiating section that contains two new chapters on selling to the Japanese customer and what to expect in meetings. The chapter on selling emphasizes developing a relationship with the customer, how to make a "soft sell," creating the right appearance and packaging of products, and conducting effective after-sales service. The chapter on meeting etiquette describes the typical Japanese meeting and features a section on how to make effective presentations.

Correspondence is an integral element of business communication. A sample business letter translated from Japanese into English is the focus of a new chapter, which provides the reader with a concrete example of how the Japanese style of correspondence differs from that traditional in America. A new chapter on greeting cards and other rituals provides advice on when to send seasonal greetings, and to whom. Finally, a new chapter on "return culture shock" deals with this difficult, yet rarely discussed, aspect of relocating. Valuable tips for the expatriate will help ease the transition back to life in the home country. The appendix materials have been updated as well and include a new section on American state offices in Japan.

The Importance of Crossing into Japanese Culture

Farsighted American business people realize that the Japanese market is one they cannot ignore and that, in order to be successful in the Japanese market, they have to understand what makes the Japanese businessman tick. It is not essential, however, that you learn and follow all the customs laid out in this book. Japanese don't expect or want you to become Japanese. The most important thing is that you become aware that unique Japanese customs exist and that you learn to use your good judgment about what behavior is most appropriate at any given time. It is in our interest to make the interaction as successful as it can be.

Many aspects of Japanese culture are as opposed to our values and our style as you could imagine. But we are in an inextricable relationship with the Japanese that would be difficult, and certainly not in our interest, to leave. The beauty of our relationship is how much we have to learn from each other. The danger is that those on both sides of the Pacific will fail to learn how to interact in a positive manner with one another, and thereby create a widening gulf between our two nations.

I haven't written this book to tell you how to behave or whether or not you should like the Japanese. I do want your actions and opinions regarding Japan to be a product of understanding and investigation, rather than misinformation, propaganda, or stereotyping. My purpose with this new edition is to provide you with objective information and advice to make your own educated judgments. If this book succeeds in raising your awareness and heightening your observation skills, it has served its purpose.

Some Kudos Are in Order

In the preparation of this book, I have had much help. For their help in the first edition, my heartfelt thanks go to Jan Works, Meg Rowland, and Elmer Luke for their constant patience, professionalism, and emotional support, and to Bob Rowland, my brother, for his technical support. My thanks also to Hori Irita, Vice President, Japan Travel Bureau, Los Angeles; Akio Takanashi, JETRO, Los Angeles; Ryuichi Kameyama, Manager, International Sales, Kintetsu Internation, Tokyo; and to Michi Swanson, Tricia Vita, Joyce Kruithof, Stella Manuel, and Stephen Benfey—not only for all their help but also for the special memories we share.

In the making of the second edition I would like to give a very special thank-you to Iwao Tomita, Senior Executive Partner, Deloitte Touche Tohmatsu, Japan; Yumi Miyamoto, San Diego State University; Christopher Engholm, Pacific Rim Ventures; and Ken Takada, Administrative Manager, Kyocera America, Inc., who have all contributed long hours of assistance. My gratitude also goes to those who made other contributions: Dr. Thomas Lifson, Management Consultant; Kathleen Hartung; Marie Benson, Manager of Japan Operations Analysis, Merck & Co.; Stephen Benfey, Ventura Associate, Inc., Tokyo; Ichiro Tsuruoka, Nippon Credit Bank Ltd.; and Douglas Brown, Far East Sales Representative, Josten's, Inc.

I

PRELIMINARIES

Putting Form and Etiquette in Perspective

Tokyo. A boardroom. Twenty minutes into a meeting. The Japanese gentlemen seated across the table from you are wearing Western business suits as stylish as your own. They're smoking Marlboros, and they nod and smile politely as the conversation continues. Two or three of them speak to you in English with ease.

You think to yourself: These are intelligent men, obviously very Westernized, with impeccable manners. You wonder why so many veterans of Japanese business dealings have warned you of the mine fields of misunderstanding and illogical behavior that await you on this, your first business trip to Japan.

It's been a long meeting, and you end it feeling confident about your prospects. But then days go by with no further communication. All your attempts to make an appointment or get phone calls returned are thwarted. Bewildered, you leave Japan and return home with no positive results to show for your investment of time and money.

What could the problem be? you wonder. Hadn't they agreed with everything you said? Hadn't you given one of your most aggressive and lucid presentations ever? In fact, you remember you felt so good at the end of the meeting that you affectionately patted one of your new Japanese friends on the back. You remember saying to him, "I'm sure you'll decide to go with us. It's a price that can't be beat, and you can see that our product is far superior to our competitors'." Your "friend" had nodded, saying, "Yes, yes," much as his negotiating team had done throughout the discussions.

Months pass with no substantial response to your inquiries.

Naturally, you're perplexed. You reassess the negotiations. What signals did you misread? What did you do wrong? How could you have blown it so badly? Were you rude without knowing it?

It is a complicated situation, but it is primarily because the Japanese appear so Westernized that we expect other fundamental similarities in their behavior—similarities that simply don't exist. Of course, Western notions have had a large impact on Japanese culture and no doubt will continue to do so. However, the Japanese have mastered the art of adopting desirable aspects of other cultures without changing their own basic values and customs, much the way an overcoat gives one a different appearance without the garments underneath having been changed.

Japanese manners have long been dictated by a highly evolved system of ethics. For a multitude of reasons, this system endures, working remarkably well within Japanese culture. For many of the same reasons, it behooves anyone having contact with the Japanese to be aware of the form and etiquette that are basic to this system of ethics. The more you know about these implicit rules of behavior, the less likely you are to misrepresent yourself or misunderstand your Japanese associates. The better versed you are in simple Japanese customs, the more favorably will you—and what you represent—be viewed. A small gesture can make a large difference.

The first thing you must realize is that for the Japanese, proper etiquette and form are of paramount importance. In the West, especially the United States, behavior is guided by an abstract code based loosely on what is generally referred to as the Judeo-Christian ethic. Westerners are disciplined by a moral sense of guilt, and in that context manners become a kind of incidental courtesy.

Japanese culture, on the other hand, has been obsessed with form and has created a strict code of behavior reinforced by the consequence of severe embarrassment if proper form is not maintained at all times. So important is this sense of form that in past centuries people were regularly beheaded for breaches of etiquette. Unlike the should-do's when in the presence of others that influence Western manners, the Japanese code at one time dictated what a person wore, what and how he ate, what he said in a given situation, and even the position in which he slept.

Comparatively speaking, things have loosened up. Nonetheless, the importance of detailed rules governing a wide range of behavior persists in modern Japan, the business world included. Not long ago a Japanese newspaper estimated corporate Japan spends $700 million a year on etiquette training.

How successfully you interact with your Japanese counterparts—in social no less than business situations—will depend greatly on how well you understand many of these rules. Rules of etiquette protect against surprise or awkward situations and help to preserve all-important surface harmony. In addition to this, lack of knowledge of the rules governing a group is a sure sign of being an outsider. This is a universal notion applying to any group, whether associated with a sport or organized as a corporation, anywhere in the world. Someone who doesn't understand the rules, written or unwritten, cannot be considered an insider. Therefore, being aware of the rules is one way of seeming less of an outsider. Additionally, knowing what is expected of you at any given time relieves you of the guesswork that may be required in a less ritualized Western society.

A few basics concept about the Japanese you should keep in mind are:

- The Japanese believe that surface harmony must be maintained at all costs.
- Form can be as, or more, important than content. How you say something is as critical as what you say.
- The Japanese have a strong aversion to confronting others in open opposition.
- The sense of obligation is a powerful motivator of Japanese behavior.
- The similarity of background and habits shared by the Japanese permit them to understand one another with very little or no verbalization.
- Cooperation among all members of a group takes precedence over individual responsibility, authority, or initiative.
- The Japanese believe that decisions based on logic alone reflect a coldness and insensitivity to human nature.

- Harmony is valued as much as, and often above, truth. The Japanese will usually avoid being frank and open when these could create discomfort or cause loss of face.
- A sense of hierarchy and status dictates what is appropriate behavior at any given time.

One of the dangers of a book that discusses the characteristics of a culture is that it could contribute to a person's tendency to stereotype. The reader must remember at all times that while a Japanese may choose to conform to his or her society more than an American would, each Japanese is still a unique individual. Any generalization is, at best, accurate only when applied to a culture at large—not to individuals. Trying to make individuals fit the stereotypes can lead to resentment and further misunderstanding.

There is, in fact, a wide spectrum of Japanese behavior. At one end of the spectrum is the very traditional; at the other is the very Westernized. Most people, however, lie somewhere in between. The trouble is that there is no set behavior for the in-between group. Sometimes they behave in a Western manner while at other times they will act in an extremely traditional manner. This variable behavior makes these Japanese very unpredictable. Some, in fact, will choose to act one way or another depending on which is most to their advantage at a given time.

Much of the focus here is on typical Japanese behavior. To attempt to explain Japanese character in all its variance and complexities would take volumes and serve a different purpose from that of this book. My objective is to acquaint you with some of the basics of form that are integral to the Japanese culture, offering at the same time as much insight as is feasible in a handbook such as this. However, it is important not to let knowledge of a "typical" Japanese person be a substitute for finding out about the individual.

To return to our Tokyo board meeting, suppose the Japanese team had been sitting on *tatami* mats, dressed in kimono, and negotiating in the Japanese language; though they would have displayed outward dissimilarities to you, you may have been pleasantly surprised you had forged a connection with people who seemed so different. Because the Japanese of today appear similar to us in so many ways, we are surprised when their hidden differences affect our business dealings with them. The aura of the Japanese being Western is what creates many of our false expectations and ensuing confusion. It is more correct, and perhaps more useful, to consider the Japanese to be "modernized" rather than Westernized.

2
Setting the
Cultural Stage

Every culture has basic values and orientations that form the foundation on which its customs are built. The more you understand these, the more the observable behaviors will make sense. While it would be out of place in a handbook such as this to dwell on these aspects, I will briefly discuss a few that directly affect how Japanese people interact with each other.

A Team Approach

A salient feature of Japanese society is its group orientation. This does not mean the Japanese are without individualism or variety. But it does mean they highly value and encourage the ability to work well within the group.

Early training is instrumental in developing this skill. Schoolchildren are assigned to a group at the beginning of the year and are expected to contribute to the progress of the group as a whole. They are encouraged to help each other and be mutually reliant. Smarter children are instructed to help those who are slower. In addition, various aspects of social behavior are evaluated and graded on primary school report cards.

One of the worst forms of punishment is being ostracized and excluded from the group. A young child may be punished by being temporarily put outside the door—isolated from the family group. Chastising children by saying that others will laugh at them is another way of emphasizing the importance of others' opinions and the need to be accepted by the collective. In Japan's group-oriented society, an individual's identity is largely defined in terms of the group.

Many Japanese, of course, feel that this sort of conformity requires compromising individual desires and demands a great deal of self-discipline. Most, however, feel the trade-off is worth it for the sense of security and order they receive in return. While at first glance it appears that individuals lose freedom in this set-up, in some ways it brings freedom. For example, the resulting social order means you are free from many of the fears prevalent in the West, such as being physically accosted or losing a job to which you have dedicated many years of your life—both relatively uncommon occurrences in Japan.

Knowing Your Place in the Hierarchy

Japanese society is also characterized by a hierarchical structure. The hierarchy within a group is, of course, significant, but so is the societal hierarchy. Following the mandate of Confucianism, teachers and bureaucrats are in the upper echelons.

The hierarchical structure dictates that due respect be afforded those of higher status. In fact, so important is the proper conveyance of respect that two Japanese can barely interact until they have determined their relative status. Because the status of a person's group is transferred to the individual, those who work for premier corporations, ministries, or universities are given highest regard. In addition to employment, other influencing factors include age, schooling, and family background. Probably most important to you, however, is that the buyer almost always has relatively higher status in the buyer-seller relationship. A notable exception would be when the seller comes from a large, powerful company and the buyer is relatively insignificant.

Displaying Respect

In order to preserve the harmony that is so essential to a group orientation, and to maintain the clarity of the hierarchy structure, showing proper respect to others becomes the vital social lubricant. The methods and opportunities to convey it are endless—and, what's more, they are in no way limited to obvious means such as using polite language. There are a multitude of subtle, polite behaviors a Japanese automatically employs when in the presence of a superior, a client, or a customer.

To help insure that their discriminating shoppers are treated with due respect, Japanese retailers put new employees through rigorous etiquette training. They know only too well that when customers have a choice they will not patronize establishments with personnel who are less than polite. Salespeople are generous with ultra-polite language that is imbued with honorifics and that repeatedly conveys humility and gratitude. They hasten to show their commitment to providing the customer with the quality he or she deserves by apologizing sincerely for anything that is less than perfect. Demure "escalator girls" wearing white gloves greet escalator riders, cautioning them to watch their step.

Exhibiting and eliciting respect is a part of everyday corporate life in Japan. When addressed by his superior, an employee will stand erect, being careful to show respect by responding in the affirmative to every request, as well as at every pause, to demonstrate he is listening attentively. If he must convey a message to a seated superior in the presence of others, he will try to physically lower himself to the same or a lower level. An employee will be careful not to walk ahead of a senior; walking slightly behind shows the proper deference. In these ways, body language conveys a message that is often much louder than words.

Showing respect is even more critical when dealing with a customer. Corporate personnel will take every opportunity to reaffirm their clients' distinguished status. They will not forget to send a thoughtful gift or card at appropriate times. Even minor details, such as hanging up the telephone as soon as they are finished talking rather than waiting for the client to disengage first, would be considered discourteous.

When Rules Disappear

Within the groups to which a Japanese belongs, there is a rigidly prescribed set of manners that one must follow. The closest circle is one's family and friends; the most remote is made up of those people one meets infrequently but regularly or for a specific purpose.

Outside these circles, however, rules of conduct are not delineated, and this is where Japanese etiquette often goes out the window. In these circumstances, where one has no formalized relationship with other people—not even the casual one between a storekeeper and a customer—there is no prescribed way to behave. It may surprise the visitor to observe Japanese who normally have impeccable manners behaving in a less than exemplary fashion. This is especially true when anonymity is certain, such as in a crowd, when blatant pushing or shoving is not uncommon and simple courtesies are sometimes forgotten. Don't assume that this rudeness is directed at you because you're a foreigner, although at times it will seem that way. It's likely that you haven't been singled out; you'll notice that shoving can be quite indiscriminate.

3
Making Contact

Business deals in Japan are thought to be more a commitment, more like a marriage, than a single transaction. Like a marriage, a business relationship is thought to last for life. For this reason, these relationships will be entered into slowly, carefully, and with the observance of traditional rituals. It follows that the Japanese have a hearty aversion to cold calls. Although cold-calling can work on rare occasions in Japan, it is the exception, not the rule. Consequently, having "connections" is the name of the game. Connections are critical to getting anything done. In fact, it would be unwise to even consider approaching a Japanese businessman or government official without going through an intermediary for that all-important introduction.

Getting one person to introduce you to another prior to a first business meeting is more than a polite custom: it is part of the ethics of Japanese business life. First of all, the Japanese feel honor-bound to welcome anyone who comes through an introduction from a common friend or an esteemed business reference. But possibly more significant is the unwritten rule that neither party will do anything that would cause the introducer to lose face. In a nonlegalistic society this is a vital means of ensuring ethical behavior.

The Right Connection

Because practically everything is done through introductions, quite possibly the most important possession to have in Japan is connections. Good Japanese universities are very difficult to get into, but, once in, students are almost guaranteed diplomas. They spend much of their time in extracurricular activities. During this period most students are building bonds with as many others as they can to begin the network that will support and enhance their careers.

In addition to investing time and energy to develop your connections, you may want to consider a couple of other related elements. Your introducer is putting himself on the line, so don't take the introduction lightly. It is important not only that you show your gratitude to him properly, but also that you take care not to discredit him in any way.

Remember, too, that you can use your connections as leverage. An unwritten part of the contract may be the introductions you can provide. This, of course, should be an asset you allude to with some subtlety.

Since the Japanese tend to be wary of anyone who approaches them without a personal introduction, any connection is better than none. But the better your introducer, the better footing you'll have from the start.

Your introducer is called a *shōkai-sha*. It is best to choose a *shōkai-sha* whose status is respected or one to whom the individual you want to meet has a sense of obligation. This person may be a superior in the same company, a close family friend or relative, an old schoolmate or professor, an important supplier to his firm, an officer of his company's bank, or a fellow member of one of the associations listed in appendix C. *Shōkai-sha* can also be hired through accounting, consulting, and law firms in the West that have branches in Japan. When you have absolutely no other choice, obtain a letter of introduction from your embassy.

The *shōkai-sha* may later act as a mediator (a *chūkai-sha*) when the negotiating gets tough. A *chūkai-sha*, who acts as a trusted and respected go-between in business affairs, may play a critical role in determining the outcome of the negotiations by exerting influence; he can also give you suggestions and feedback along the way.

It would be wise to have your *shōkai-sha* sound out the company you wish to approach to see if it is even interested. Otherwise, many frustrating months may pass before it becomes apparent the company was never interested but felt compelled to go through the motions to fulfill a sense of obligation to the introducer.

Someone who has held a government office can be particularly useful to you if dealing with the bureaucracy is likely to be a problem. For this same reason, former government officials are often hired by companies. Called *amakudari* (descendants from heaven), they are the rare exception of personnel who are hired into a Japanese company at the top, rather than coming up through the ranks.

The *shōkai-sha* will expect some sort of return for his trouble. This could be direct payment, or a piece of the action in the event you are successful. For those who do not expect payment, you may still want to show your gratitude in some tangible way. Consider presenting him with an appropriately expensive gift, inviting him to an exclusive restaurant and nightclub, or treating him to a few days at a famous golf resort in your country. In some situations you may just "owe him one." What is appropriate compensation will depend upon your relationship and the importance of the introduction.

Ideally, the introduction should be performed in person. When that is not possible or appropriate, the introducer should call the targeted person on your behalf, write a letter of introduction, or, at the very least, write a note of endorsement on his business card.

Who's the Boss?

Even if you manage to get an introduction to the individual who appears, by his title or place on the organization chart, to have the final decision-making responsibility, there is another obstacle to overcome—the *ringi* system of sharing authority. (This is discussed in more detail in chapter 14.)

The group approach to management that is practiced by most medium and large Japanese companies may be a very democratic system, but it makes it hard to figure out who has ultimate authority. Usually there is no *one* individual "in charge." Managers share responsibility—the larger the company and the project proposed, the more sections or departments are involved in the decision. Most likely you will have to meet and deal with all of them to accomplish your objective.

The following diagram shows the way someone is introduced with a business card.

TARGET PERSON

NAME   **TITLE**   **MESSAGE**

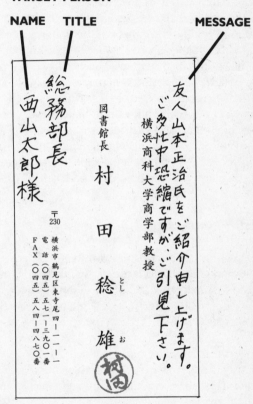

The message reads, "I am introducing my friend, Yamamoto Shōji. I apologize for bothering you at such a busy time, but please meet him."

It may be signed by the introducer or he may affix his personal seal. The protocol is to put it in a special envelope and write the target person's name and address on it. The introducer should then call ahead to the target person to let him know he will be receiving a call from the introducee.

Seniority is key to this aspect of Japanese management. Usually it counts more than intelligence, leadership, or problem-solving ability, although this is slowly changing. The thing to remember is that you must cultivate your connections among a company's middle managers (section head to department head) as well as top management, because middle managers will be important players involved in the decision-making process and will have influence in shaping the opinions of top management. Also not to be ignored are lower-level personnel who may very well play a critical role in the way they present the research they perform on your proposal. This is not to imply it would not be useful to have higher-level executives of the two companies meet for a formal *aisatsu* (greeting). Especially if the venture proposed is of significant magnitude, this is an essential step in setting the tone of the relationship. It is, however, more of a formality than an opportunity to discuss details of your proposal.

A *"Shōsha" Shōkai*

One feature of the Japanese business structure that may be confusing to the uninitiated is the existence of large trading companies (*sōgō-shōsha*) that handle much of Japan's trade and generally keep the wheels of commerce well greased. Although there are thousands of *shōsha* in Japan, fewer than a dozen of the largest of them handle more than half of Japan's import/export trade. (See appendix C for more on trading companies.)

You may choose to have one of these general trading companies or a smaller specialized trading company facilitate your entrée into the Japanese market. If not, finding out whether the company you are approaching is affiliated with a major *sōgō-shōsha* and subsequently its industrial/financial group is vitally important. Sources, such as JETRO and reference books, for researching the affiliations of various companies and *sōgō-shōsha* are provided in the appendices.

4
Meeting People

As elsewhere in the world, Japanese business people try to size each other up during a first meeting. They may, however, use different criteria than you are accustomed to in formulating their first impression of you. If this meeting is important, it is in your interest to know what these standards are.

The key to a good first impression is to make things go as smoothly as possible. Your safest tactic is to take your cues from the person you are meeting. He may be trying hard to be "Western," in which case it would be most polite to accommodate his efforts. However, if he has not had much exposure to the West and greets you in the Japanese manner, you'll achieve the most points by being able to reciprocate according to his style.

The Japanese Greeting

When meeting someone for the first time in Japan, it is proper to say your name and the name of your company, even if you are introduced and even if this means repeating what an introducer has said. A Japanese would usually say something equivalent to "I'm Jones of Global Trading." He would then say something to the effect, "It's very nice to meet you and I look forward to a friendly relationship." (See chapter 11 if you would like to learn this opening gambit in Japanese.)

You may have noticed that first names are rarely used in Japan except within the family and with very close personal friends. It can, therefore, be rather shocking to a Japanese when an American says, "Hiroshi, just call me Joe." This violates the sense of formality and group orientation. It would be much more acceptable to use last names both for yourself and your Japanese acquaintance. When both first and last names are indicated in Japanese, the family name comes first and the given name second. However, when speaking in English they will usually reverse their names for your benefit.

Japanese frequently use titles in place of the other party's name as it shows respect for their status. For example, when addressing a high-level client, you would call him Mr. President (*shachō-san*), Director (*senmu*), and so on. Even outside of business it's common to use *sensei* when speaking to a teacher or doctor and *okusan* when addressing someone's wife.

If your Japanese counterpart has spent time abroad, he may have taken on Western customs and may introduce himself using his first name. In that case, by all means use first names. But unless he or she requests or initiates it, it's safer not to presume. Even in the event that you establish a first-name relationship outside Japan, it would be wise to revert back to using his last name in front of his Japanese colleagues to avoid embarrassment.

Be sure to attach "Mr." or "Ms." to their names, or the Japanese suffix *san* (as in Tanaka-*san*), which has a similar meaning. Please keep in mind, however, that *san* is an honorific and therefore should not be used with your own name or when referring to your spouse or your children, or to someone in your company when talking with someone outside of it. In other words, when calling someone in another company, you would ask the receptionist, for example, if Suzuki-*san* were there. She would reply, "I'm sorry, Suzuki is not in the office at the moment." This is because it is considered rude to elevate people of your own group when speaking with someone outside of it. Honorifics are for the other party. Of course, when Mr. Suzuki returns she would say to him, "Suzuki-*san*, you had a phone call." Now Suzuki has become "the other party."

When speaking in English it is perfectly acceptable to use Mr. with a name instead of *san*. However, if your Japanese counterpart has not had much experience abroad, you might want to use only your last name without Mr. attached to avoid confusion.

The Business Card

For the Japanese, a person's business card is an identifying tool that does far more than conveniently convey a way to get in touch later. The position of the person and the status of the company he works for are vitally important as indicators of how others should comport themselves with him. For example, one might show greater respect to a junior executive of IBM than to a senior executive of a smaller, less powerful company. Cards are therefore exchanged at every opportunity and with a fair degree of ceremony.

The first thing you will want to do is to make sure you take several hundred with you on a trip to Japan. You will be surprised at how quickly they disappear and it is unacceptable to run out. Be sure to carry your cards *wherever* you go.

Some people in the United States are in the habit of inserting a few stray cards in their wallet. To the Japanese, however, reaching to your rear side for your credentials (or putting their card in your rear pocket) is thought to be crude. You should place your cards in a distinctive case and carry it in the front inside pocket of your jacket. If you are going to be meeting people for the first time, expect to exchange cards and have them ready so you don't have to search for them. Make sure they are clean, without pen corrections or notes. If you want to give someone your hotel number, have it handy, but don't have it written on your card. Women may carry cards in a purse, but should also keep them in a nice case that is readily accessible.

Unless you are seated in a *tatami* mat room, you should be standing when you give your card. To show the greatest respect, avoid having anything, such as a chair, plant, or table, between you and the other person. Give your card carefully with your right or both hands, and, by all means, don't deal your cards out as though you are playing poker.

Giving or receiving anything with two hands elevates the other person. Keep this in mind when meeting a Japanese of much higher rank than yourself or a potentially important customer. Even if you have not been able to use two hands during the exchange, it is polite to hold the other party's card with both hands or in your right hand, resting the card on your left.

Japanese who do business with foreigners will usually have an

English translation on the reverse side of their cards, but the translation may not be exact. Because there is no standard translation of the Japanese titles or positions within and among companies, you may be confused about the rank and management level of the person you have just met. It would therefore be worthwhile to study the Japanese titles or to have someone interpret them for you.

Below are two lists: one of a typical Japanese corporate hierarchy and one of the names of places and departments in a typical organizational structure. Not only are English translations not standardized, but there is no consistent hierarchical order of some of these positions among Japanese companies. For example, in some companies *jichō* is below the rank of *buchō* and in others it is above. However, even the English translation can also be misleading, since the titles are not strictly equivalent. For example, Japanese companies generally have only one vice-president, whereas an American company may have many. For these reasons, it becomes all the more important that you learn something about the Japanese company's organizational structure.

TYPICAL CORPORATE HIERARCHY

会長	Kaichō	Chairman
副会長	Fuku Kaichō	Vice Chairman
社長	Shachō	President
副社長	Fuku Shachō	Vice President
専務取締役	Senmu Torishimariyaku	Senior Executive/ Managing Director
常務取締役	Jōmu Torishimariyaku	Managing Director

取締役	Torishimariyaku	Director
監査役	Kansayaku	Statutory Auditor
相談役	Sōdanyaku	Senior Advisor
支店長	Shitenchō	Branch Manager
部長	Buchō	Department/Division Manager
次長	Jichō	Deputy Director
副部長	Fuku Buchō	Vice Department Manager
部長代理	Buchō Dairi	Deputy Department Manager
部長補佐	Buchō Hosa	Assistant Department Manager
課長	Kachō	Section Head
課長代理	Kachō Dairi	Deputy Section Head
課長補佐	Kachō Hosa	Assistant Section Head
係長	Kakarichō	Supervisor (Subsection Head)
係長補佐	Kakarichō Hosa	Assistant Supervisor
班長	Hanchō	Group Leader
職長	Shokuchō	Foreman

主任	Shunin	Project Head
社員	Shain	Employee

TYPICAL ORGANIZATIONAL STRUCTURE

取締役会	Torishimariyaku Kai	Board of Directors
本部／本社	Honbu/Honsha	Headquarters
部	Bu	Department
室	Shitsu	Office
課	Ka	Section
総務部	Sōmu-bu	General Affairs
経理部	Keiri-bu	Accounting Department
調査部	Chōsa-bu	Business Research Department
企画室	Kikaku-shitsu	Corporate Planning Office
技術部	Gijyutsu-bu	Engineering Department
財務部	Zaimu-bu	Finance Department
法務部	Hōmu-bu	Legal Department

人事部	Jinji-bu	Personnel Department
生産管理部	Seisankanri-bu	Production Control Department
商品開発室	Shōhin Kaihatsu-shitsu	Product Development Office
広報部	Kōhō-bu	Public Relations Department
購買部	Kōbai-bu	Purchasing Department
秘書室	Hisho-shitsu	Secretariat

After receiving a business card, you should take time to read it carefully and comment on something contained in it, if you can (such as the logo, the address, or the person's position), before carefully putting it away. To not read it is to imply the person is not important. Also, by reading it, you may gain valuable information about the person's status, which will be a determining factor in how much respect you need to show. Far from being uncomfortable with status differences, Japanese will search for the element that clarifies who has the higher rank.

If the person you have received a card from is of higher status than you (or is your customer), you should not put his card away before he puts yours away. During a meeting, it's quite acceptable to place the cards you've received in front of you to help you remember people's names. Collecting the cards is a sure sign that the discussion is over.

Because to the Japanese the business card is a personal representation, it is critical that you treat it with respect. Do not write on it in front of the person unless you ask him first—and only if you have a good reason, such as clarifying something that is not translated into English. Later you may wish to make many identifying and incidental notes about the person, but don't deface his card in his presence.

Observing the rituals of hierarchy, people are introduced in order of rank—from the highest level to the lower level. Conversely, when introducing two people, the person of lower status is presented to the higher one ("Director, may I present Mr. Satō?"), rather than the reverse. The person of lower status usually initiates the card exchange. Of course, if you come at someone's invitation, the host will often proffer his first.

These courtesies are especially important for someone in sales. However, if you are meeting someone of much higher status than yourself, offering your card without him or her offering first is considered presumptuous. People of superior status are treated a little like royalty and often do not even carry a card; a subordinate will frequently carry cards for them.

It is, of course, good form to have your card translated into Japanese on the back. It is imperative to have it translated at a reputable place and advisable to have it proofread by a Japanese who understands your job function.

I'm sure by now a book could be written about humorous translation disasters (for example, Head of Light Guides Technology Department translated as Chief Lighthouse Keeper). While these make good party stories, they do not add to your credibility and could lead to severe embarrassment later if your counterparts grossly misunderstand your position.

It is important to hand your card so the receiver can read it without turning it around. This means that you need to know which is the top and which is the bottom. Traditionally, Japanese is written vertically, from top to bottom, right to left, but it is now popular to have cards printed horizontally from left to right. If you have yours printed horizontally, make sure that the top is the same for both languages, so you can easily tell which way is up. Another help would be to have a logo in the same position on both sides. (Refer to appendix A to locate a printer in your area who will print business cards in Japanese.)

The size of Japanese business cards is a little larger than ours ($3\frac{1}{2}'' \times 2''$), but it is not critical that you adhere to this standard.

The First Meeting

Because Japan is a nonlegalistic society, a business relationship that is built on friendship and trust is generally valued more than one that depends on the best price or other practical considerations. Japanese businessmen are generally willing to spend time and money on the preliminaries, on getting to know you.

They will be looking for signs of sincerity, compatibility, and trustworthiness. In this sense, sincerity means you sincerely want to do business with them, to the point that you won't drag out the lawyers if something needs to be changed. Compatibility means that you are interested in their well-being, not just in making money. And trustworthiness means they can trust you to protect them from losing face. The Japanese want to develop personal ties that will help the business relationship continue through times that may not be as profitable for one party as was the case initially.

Your behavior at this first meeting is critical. Again, your status in relationship to the person you are meeting is the determining factor. If you are of lower status, you don't have to be obsequious, but you are expected to be deferential. If you are of higher status, you should act accordingly. You shouldn't be arrogant, but neither should you try to become buddies with those of lower (or higher rank) than you. Be polite and be formal. Later you can let your Japanese counterparts take the lead in indicating the proper level of informality.

The usual general topics of conversations—the weather, mutual friends, your impressions of Japan, your flight over, hobbies, golf and other sports—are good starters that help put people at ease. Reading a local newspaper as soon as you arrive in Japan will help to give you conversation topics. Also be prepared to discuss general information about your company, such as corporate philosophy and organizational structure, including where you and your department fit in.

Eventually, sharing personal things, such as wallet photos of your children, helps to build a sense of closeness. Even when the subject of the family is broached, it's better not to ask questions in much detail. An older Japanese businessman in particular may leave all domestic matters to his wife and not know such details as what his child is studying in college. You wouldn't want to put him on the spot by asking a question he can't answer.

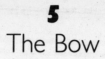

5
The Bow

One of the first things you may notice on a trip to Japan is how frequently people bow to each other. A survey done by a Japanese magazine revealed that a typical businessman may bow 200 to 300 times a day, while a department store escalator girl who greets approaching customers may bow 2,000 to 3,000 times a day. A bow can be performed while standing or when kneeling, in Japanese fashion, if one is sitting in a Japanese-style *tatami* room.

The basic ingredient in a bow is humility. You elevate, or honor, the other person by humbling yourself. The lower you bow, the more you honor the other party. Probably one of the most versatile human gestures, a bow can be used to convey numerous sentiments. For example, a superior can instantly communicate that a discussion is over with a quick bow.

To Bow or Not to Bow?

The older the Japanese, the more formal and traditional they usually are. Remember, however, that many Japanese will be prepared to follow the Western custom of shaking hands, so try to remain flexible and take your cue from your Japanese counterpart. If you feel he is uncomfortable, wondering whether to shake your hand or not, then by all means extend your hand. Japanese also often bow and shake hands at the same time.

Do keep in mind, though, that since shaking hands is not a traditional part of their culture, it would be unwise to judge a Japanese on the firmness of his handshake in the way we might in the West. In general, they tend to dislike strong handshakes. A weak handshake on his part may simply reflect this attitude. By the same token, a very strong handshake from you might send a more aggressive message than you would like.

Uses of the Bow

Unless you are experienced and comfortable with bowing, don't initiate a bow. You won't be expected to as it's not your custom. However, since protocol requires that a bow always be returned, make some attempt to do so. To not return a bow is akin to refusing a handshake. (It is not necessary to bow back to personnel at establishments such as department stores and restaurants who bow to welcome you.)

To illustrate what an automatic gesture this is, a friend of mine relayed an experience he had when leaving his Los Angeles hotel to go for a run. He came jogging down the front steps decked out in the latest runner's fashion. Without slowing his pace he bent over to miss an opened window as he made a right at the base of the stairs. At the same time, he happened to look up to his left. There stood a gaggle of Japanese businessmen who had just disembarked from their tour bus surrounded by heaps of luggage. To his surprise they all politely returned his "bow."

You may discover many unexpected uses for the bow yourself. If you find yourself in a department store where everyone seems too shy to help a foreigner, you can give a little bow when someone glances your way. Chances are she will bow back out of reflex and once she has, she is obligated to help you.

USES OF THE BOW

For greetings and partings:
  Introductions
  Welcomes
  Acknowledgment of another's presence
  Gaining attention
For sincerity:
  Offering assistance, food, presents, etc.
  Showing gratitude
  Congratulating
  Sympathy
For humility:
  Requests
  Apology
  Respect
For ceremony:
  Onset of events such as negotiation, competition
  Closing of events
To acknowledge or show agreement

How Low Do You Go?

The person of lower status usually initiates the bow, bows low-est, and is the last to rise. The actual depth of the bows depend upon the occasion and the relative status of the two parties.

The most frequent bow is an informal 15 degrees, held for just one or two seconds. A deeper bow is used for a superior or for a formal occasion such as a first meeting. It is usually about 30 degrees but sometimes even lower, and is held for about three seconds. Men usually leave their hands at their sides while bowing, but women usually place them on their thighs with their fingertips overlapping, or at least touching. Heels should be touching.

It is not critical that you try to get the exact degree correct. Any level of bow will be better than no bow. Japanese people appreciate your effort, so find your own comfort zone. (If, however, you are attempting to convey sincere gratitude or regret, a very low bow will express that more completely than the accompanying words.) Bows should be controlled, deliberate actions, not a bobbing up and down.

If you rise from your bow and find the other person hasn't yet, you should bow again to acknowledge the expression of respect. On most occasions, especially when saying good-bye, there will be more than one bow. It's not unusual to see a Japanese bowing while speaking on the phone, or an old lady bowing repeatedly to another lady in a departing bus even after they are out of each other's sight.

In a *Tatami* Room

The ritual for meeting or greeting someone while kneeling in a *tatami* mat room may be useful to know. You can never tell when you'll be invited to a traditional-style celebration at a Japanese restaurant, and if you are meeting an important person the salutation may indeed be formal. Kneeling bows are executed by placing the hands on the *tatami* about five inches apart and lowering the head to within five inches of the floor for a deep bow. The business cards will be slid across the *tatami*.

You should not sit on a cushion until after the introduction has taken place and only after the host or hostess has insisted you do so. When someone else comes to greet you, you must again remove yourself from the cushion to perform the bow—to do otherwise would be like remaining seated while shaking hands with a person who is standing.

6
Hosting Japanese Guests

Those who have had the pleasure of being a guest of the Japanese can attest to the red-carpet treatment they invariably bestow. The Japanese people have mastered the art of making guests feel honored, if not out-and-out pampered. For this reason it is advisable that you not cut corners when you are the host. Doing so could convey the message that you don't feel your guests are important.

Taking time to have a fruit basket sent to your guest's hotel room is well worth the effort if you wish to communicate that he is valued. Before he arrives, ask the hotel to make sure he is not booked into a room numbered four or forty-four. Four is a homonym for death and therefore is often omitted in Japanese hotels and hospitals, just as thirteen often is in the West.

A Japanese would certainly feel remiss in his obligations as a host if he did not plan activities for his guests for all nonbusiness hours, including evenings and weekends. It is considered the height of negligence to leave someone to their own devices, especially in a foreign country. This can sometimes make Westerners visiting Japan feel positively suffocated. But Japanese guests, who are not used to much time by themselves, will probably not appreciate your offer to give them a "free day," unless perhaps to shop for presents to take back home to Japan, in which case they still may need much assistance. If you are unable to spend this much time with them personally, try to arrange for someone else to fill in when you are not available.

You should not host people of higher status than yourself. Such a situation conveys that your company does not find the guest important. If you are courting a company and find that a person of higher rank than yourself is part of their delegation, try to get someone in your company of equal or higher status to do the hosting.

During nonbusiness activities, try to match rank for rank. Informal relationships are best formed at equal level. To facilitate bonding between individuals, the Japanese group can be divided up for certain activities. Executives can be taken for rounds of golf while underlings are taken shopping.

When Japanese guests are passengers in your car, make sure to seat them according to their rank.

Dining

Before making restaurant plans, it is good to find out the culinary preferences of important guests. Lower-level personnel can often provide this sort of information as they frequently make arrangements for their superiors. They can tell you whether their boss likes to try new cuisine or whether he is happiest with fish and rice, much like a "meat and potatoes man" in America. If the latter is true, a highly respected Chinese or French restaurant would be a good choice. (Unless you are very familiar with Japanese customs, hosting guests at a Japanese restaurant could make you vulnerable to committing faux pas and appearing uncultured. Additionally, at such a restaurant, the Japanese may feel that they should be hosting you.) Request a private dining room whenever practical.

Since beef is expensive in Japan, your guests may appreciate the opportunity to dine at a steak house. Unless they request it, however, it's probably advisable not to schedule steak two nights in a row. For people who are not used to eating it in large quantities, meat can be overwhelming to the system.

More adventuresome types may enjoy a local delicacy or traditional dish. A famous restaurant is almost always an appropriate choice for either category.

CAR PROTOCOL

When a chauffeur is driving, the highest-ranked Japanese should be the first to enter and the last to exit, sitting right behind the driver, unless your guest chooses otherwise.

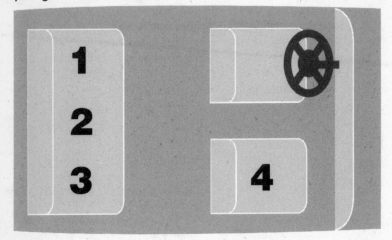

When a colleague is driving, the highest-ranking seat is next to the driver in the front seat.

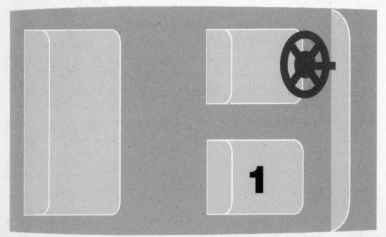

Observing Some Etiquette

In Japan there is a strict hierarchial seating arrangement. The most honored person should be seated the furthest from the door. When hosting a group, seat the guests on the side that faces the door and hosts with their backs to the door. Top people will usually be seated in the middle. In a more informal setting you may want to seat your Japanese guests next to their American counterparts of the same level so that they will have the opportunity to get to know each other.

Try to pay the bill discreetly. Since the time of the samurai, money has been thought to be somewhat course or crude. As a guest in Japan, you will almost never see a bill. Arrangements are made ahead of time or an underling takes care of it.

After the Dinner

In the case of corporate guests, dinner should be followed by a nightclub. If you are entertaining an important person, it should be an exclusive establishment. In Japan entertaining often goes well into the night and includes three or more places in an evening. The idea is that by the end of the evening, your guests will know something about your character and strong personal bonds will have been cemented.

Hosting in Japan

If you are hosting Japanese in Japan, make sure you don't leave anyone important out. When you extend your invitation, ask a close contact if there is anyone else who should be included. Remember, though, that entertaining in Japan is very expensive. If you are on a visit there it may be better to let them take care of any socializing (unless they are your client), and you can reciprocate when they visit your country. If they have invited you, it is not necessary to offer to pay.

To avoid the problem of your Japanese guests feeling they

RESTAURANT SEATING

WINDOW

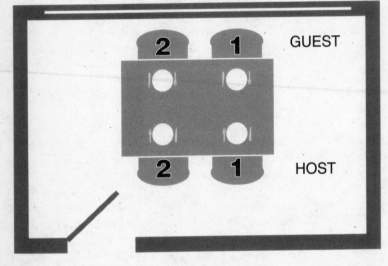

WINDOW

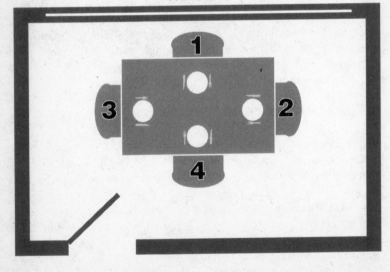

RECEPTION ROOM

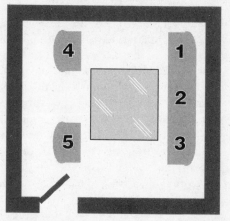

Couches are considered better than chairs, and chairs with arms are better than those without. Lower-level personnel sit closest to the door while higher-level people sit further from the door, although the senior person may choose to sit in the middle.

should be hosting you in their country, invite them to an eatery that is distinctly Western (such as the Tokyo American Club, if you are a member, or the Tokyo location of a famous restaurant of your country) so that it seems to be more your turf than theirs.

Rather than risk inviting guests to a nightclub you are not very familiar with (prices can be extravagant and unpredictable at many), it would be safer to entertain them in a hotel lounge where prices are clear.

Receiving Guests at Your Office

When Japanese guests arrive, it's probably better to receive them in a conference room than in your office. Be sure to welcome them and show some personal interest by thanking them for the visit and inquiring about their accommodations.

Try to perceive their needs before they have to ask, and take care of these whenever you can. In other words, rather than ask, "Would you like me to call ahead for you and make a reservation?" say, "I will call ahead for you." If they are carrying something heavy say, "I'll carry it for you" rather than, "Would you like me to carry it?" Directly stating one's wishes is considered rude in Japan, as the other person may not be able to accommodate your request. You should be aware that your guests may not openly state their desires.

Be sure to serve them a refreshment. If you are already drinking a cup of coffee in your own office, don't carry it into the conference room with you. You should be drinking out of the same type of cups or glasses as your guests. Honor them by showing respect for the formality of the occasion.

Be aware that while Americans typically have a "help yourself" attitude, most other countries adhere to the tradition of "be my guest." Hosts are expected to cater to their visitors. For example, you must offer your guests cream and sugar for their coffee; they will probably not reach across the table for it. Even after you have served a refreshment, Japanese people usually will not partake of it until invited to do so. Hosts wait until guests begin to pick up teacups before picking up their own, and subordinates begin drinking after their superiors.

It is not necessary to ask Japanese guests what they would like, and they would probably politely decline anyway. Simply serve what you think is appropriate. Even if they don't like what you serve, they appreciate the thought or the intention. Effort really does count in Japan.

When walking through your building, stay slightly ahead of your guests to show them the way. If an elevator is unattended, enter it first and hold the door for them. Hold it open again while they exit first.

When your guests leave, it is important to see them off. Wait until they are completely out of sight. They will almost always turn to bow or wave good-bye one last time, and it is a major breach of etiquette to have already disappeared. If they will be meeting with someone else in your company, escort them to their next destination.

Entertaining in Your Home

Although it is not commonly done in Japan, you may feel free to invite your Japanese guests to your home if you would like. However, such an invitation may lose its sense of importance if it's offered on the first meeting; it will feel more like a special event if the invitation is extended on a subsequent meeting.

Since the kitchen is considered a work room in Japan, this is not a respectable place to entertain. Older Japanese men in particular may feel uncomfortable in a kitchen. If you have a kitchen and dining room combined as one, try to serve your meal in the living room. Make them more comfortable by familiarizing them with the protocol for eating unusual foods.

While Japanese may be curious about American homes, they may also feel awkward being escorted through bedrooms. Rather than presuming and giving them "the tour," it would be better to give them the option by saying, "I'd be glad to show you the house if you would like to see it."

Good Manners Set You Apart

You may have noticed that many of the points mentioned in this chapter are not peculiar to the Japanese but would be considered good manners anywhere. Being as polite as you know how to be is always a safe course when you don't know what someone else would consider proper—and is the most anyone expects of you on your own turf. Unfortunately what has come to be acceptable behavior in America falls conspicuously short of what would be considered common manners in Japan. Being at least a cut above "common" is what separates you from the rest of the pack in the eyes of the Japanese.

II

COMMUNICATION

7
The Meaning Behind the Statement

Understanding the way people speak in their own language is critical to being able to interpret what they are trying to convey when they speak in yours. Without this knowledge we tend to assume a foreign person's words carry the same meaning as if they were used by a native speaker.

Understand Ten

One of the major differences in the ways of communicating in Japan and most English-speaking countries is the Japanese implicit style. In explicit societies such as ours, the speaker does not assume the listener understands the context behind what is being discussed and therefore provides background information with each communication. Everything is said as explicitly as possible, leaving very little to be understood by implication. People in explicit societies tend to have isolated pools of knowledge, choosing not to clutter their minds, or the issue, with more information than they need.

On the other hand, the Japanese society is considered to be an implicit one. This is epitomized in the Japanese proverb, "Say one, understand ten." For each point expressed, the listener is expected to understand nine others by implication. Because the most important portion of the conversation is often left unspoken, it becomes the responsibility of the listener to pick up on what has been implied or otherwise indicated nonverbally. This can work only when the listener understands the context of what is being discussed.

In Japan, each person is responsible for keeping himself informed. This is probably why Japanese newspapers have a daily circulation of 34 million, one of the highest in the world. About 75 percent of Japanese television broadcasting is information oriented: news, education, cultural events, and information-related quiz shows. Japanese saturate themselves with information. Having your own office would isolate you from the flow of information; it's thought to be much better to work in an open office space where you are in the middle of the information current.

An oblique method of communication works well in Japan because, as an island country, it has always enjoyed racial homogeneity and a common language, religion, and value system. Just as members of a family can, the Japanese are able, to a great degree, to anticipate the intentions and thoughts of one another.

Keep the Harmony

Because Japanese society places so much importance on the outward appearance of harmony, their language has developed in such a way as to allow very vague forms of expression. The idea is that by not making direct statements, one has a better chance of not offending anyone. Conversations begin with superficialities, so be patient about hearing the message.

Many things are said purely for the sake of etiquette and are not meant to be taken literally. For example, managers may say to those below them, "Do not hesitate to express your own opinion." You may frequently hear, "Please drop by my house anytime." Expressions like these are usually used without any real intent behind them—as Westerners can well understand. "It was a pleasure to meet you," we say, whether it was or not.

The tradition of self-effacement can also be misleading. Statements like "I am not very confident I can do it," "I am the president of a very small company," "I hold a very insignificant position," or "I'm sure I cannot do this job very well" should not be taken literally.

Conversely, foreigners should be careful not to brag, lest they make their counterparts feel inferior. It's best to avoid remarks such as "I have a beautiful wife" or "I am very proud of my achievements." However, "Our company is very proud of . . ." is fine as it reflects company spirit rather than personal vanity.

What the Japanese Mean by Yes

The word *hai* (yes) can present another dangerous trap. It is often used to let the speaker know that one is listening and not necessarily to indicate agreement or understanding. Etiquette dictates that the listener continually show he is being attentive by saying *hai*, giving nods, or making affirmative sounds. When listening to a superior, Japanese will sometimes make these interjections every few seconds. Resist the temptation to attach any meaning to them other than courtesy. Warning: Listen to the full answer before deciding what the person is saying.

Honne and *Tatemae*—Essence and Form

Understanding the meaning of, and the difference between, the concepts *honne* and *tatemae* is critical to understanding a fundamental aspect of Japanese communication. The word *honne* refers to the truth that you feel inside, or the actual truth, your true intention. *Tatemae* is your public stance, what you do or say for the sake of principle, how you would like things to be, or maybe what you think the other person would like to hear. It is a protective "front," a kind of public mask that fulfills social, corporate, and political expectations.

This discrepancy in what is thought and what is said is, of course, not unfamiliar. At times, we all compromise the truth, often in the form of "little white lies," for the sake of harmony. We might tell someone their expensive new outfit is nice or interesting even if we find it unattractive. The Japanese, however, feel compelled to make the compromise on a frequent basis as there is a constant concern for saving face and maintaining harmony. People often suppress the real or whole truth while presenting a partial truth or even saying something that hardly resembles the truth.

In the Japanese way of thinking, there may be more than one truth. For example, one truth may be that they want to do business with you, and this may be the *tatemae* you hear. However, the *honne* truth may be that they cannot. Remember it's our Judeo-Christian ethic that encourages us to see things in black and white. Things are either right or wrong, good or bad, true or false. But to most Asians things are not black and white but mostly shades of gray. What is right, good, or true is seen as highly dependent upon the circumstances surrounding the event and the perspective of the observer.

You can see how essential it is to find out what the *honne* is. Your go-between may be a good source of information. If he doesn't already know, he can probably find out more easily than you. If you have already established an informal relationship with one of your counterparts, you may be able to get a more honest opinion from him after several drinks. Lower-level personnel may have an easier time getting to *honne* than high-level executives.

Once you find out what the *honne* is, you must find a way to satisfy it without compromising the *tatemae*.

How the Japanese Say No

The Japanese rarely say no bluntly and directly. To the Japanese, a blunt no seems as if you are saying "no" to the person himself rather than to his idea, opinion, or request. With this in mind, it's easy to understand why flat denials are considered detrimental to good human relationships and why some sort of *tatemae* response might be given.

Even while presenting a *tatemae* response, though, the Japanese will often be giving you clues, leaving bread crumbs to let you know what their true feelings are or what the *honne* is. The problem arises when we take everything they say at face value and think that because they said yes, they must mean yes. Remember they may have been trying to say no in a way that would save face for you and possibly for themselves as well.

They may simply apologize, keep quiet, ask you why you want to know, become vague, or answer with a euphemism for no.

The sound "sahhh," drawn out, or the sucking in of air through the teeth usually means difficulty. A hand on the back of the neck can also indicate a problem.

If you don't pay close attention to these cues, you might miss several crucial steps and go home congratulating yourself on a deal that will never be consummated.

Apologies

Apologies are common in Japan. They show one's desire to atone for not meeting another's expectations. When fault is not an issue, they show one's sense of empathy and responsibility. Japanese usually do not link an apology directly with an excuse, so that it will not appear they feel they were justified in letting the other party down, whatever the reason.

In the United States people often avoid apologizing because they fear a lawsuit. In Japan, apologizing does not necessarily make you liable. Very often it is all the other party desires and could, in fact, save you a costly lawsuit.

I know of an American who was held by the police in Tokyo for several hours after hitting a cyclist with his car although the cyclist was not hurt. The American had not offered an apology because it had not been his fault. To the Japanese, however, this showed a lack of empathy, and they detained him for hours. Once he did apologize he was immediately released.

Sometimes the Japanese side will apologize to show regret for a problem or misunderstanding, but they may also expect an apology from you. Being polite doesn't mean they think they were at fault.

In fact, trading apologies is a good way of putting mistakes behind you and strengthening a relationship. You can ingratiate yourself by apologizing when there is really nothing to apologize for. For example, if you present something right on time to meet a deadline you can still apologize for not presenting it sooner.

A Multi-Level Language

One distinct difference between our two languages is the multiple levels of formality that exist in the Japanese language. In Japanese a different set of words may be used depending upon the relationship, relative status, and gender of the conversants. Unless you know the position of the person to whom you are speaking, this can be problematic and is the primary reason business cards are so essential.

When speaking to a superior, one uses a respectful level of language, referring to oneself with humility. The superior in turn uses an appropriate level of language. Family and close friends use another level of language, while associates of equal status use yet another. Male speech differs from female speech.

Compliments

Compliments of the kind we're accustomed to in the West are not common in Japan. Statements such as "That was a terrific presentation you gave" or "Once again, Mr. Tanaka has given us an outstanding proposal to pursue" will make your Japanese counterparts uncomfortable. These compliments, by their nature, invite comparisons and lower the status of others. Of course, support and encouragement are important, but they should be given to the group as a whole or, when given to an individual, delivered very subtly.

However, the Japanese will often directly praise someone they consider to be outside the group even when (or perhaps especially when) it's not true. For example, they will often say, "Your Japanese is so good" to foreigners who are obviously stumbling along.

In Japan a professional would probably not welcome a compliment regarding an expected accomplishment in his field. It's something like implying that he had done well in spite of no talent or pride in his work. This is especially true if the person is a superior; it indicates that you are evaluating him. It would be better to say something like, "I learned a great deal from your book" or "I would like my people to hear your ideas," rather than "Your book was a masterpiece, Professor Yamada."

Praise in Japan is often more indirect and modest than in the

West. For example, the giver of the compliment in Japan will frequently express his or her own limitations rather than say anything directly aggrandizing to the other person. In the workplace, probably the most common form of compliment is to ask the person's opinion on something.

Another way to express a compliment is in the form of gratitude. One might say, "Your husband is an inspiration to me" rather than, "Your husband is a very brilliant man." Lavish praise of any sort is considered insincere.

Casual compliments on a Japanese acquaintance's appearance can sometimes seem too personal to them. On the other hand, among close friends, Japanese may make comments on another's physique that we would find embarrassing.

The Western habit of receiving a compliment with "Thank you, I like it too," can seem quite vain. From childhood the Japanese are taught that modesty and self-deprecation are highly admirable qualities. Therefore, embarrassment is a common reaction to compliments. Bowing, smiling, or denying the validity of the compliment are the most common responses. Denying a compliment made to oneself is considered a proper demonstration of humility and consequently does not threaten good feelings the way saying no in other ways might.

A simple, sincere "Thank you," however, on the part of a Westerner receiving a compliment would probably be well taken by Japanese. There is no need to act in a manner that is unnatural to you, but keep your behavior as modest as you comfortably can.

Criticism

By and large, the Japanese are likely to be more sensitive than Westerners to personal criticism, even if they are more passive in their defense of it. At all times it is important that you be conscious of the need to save face for the person with whom you're dealing. The degree of embarrassment caused by face-to-face criticism, especially in the presence of others, would probably surprise you. In extreme cases, it can provoke such reactions as suicide or a lifetime spent seeking revenge.

Here are some ways you can criticize without being overly direct:

- Use a third party to convey your criticism gently.
- Show your dissatisfaction in a nonverbal way (such as silence).
- Be grateful and complimentary first, but show some reservation by ending your sentence with "but ..." Then let the person slowly pull it out of you.
- Go out drinking together and bring the matter up in the second or third hour of filling each other's sake cups.

Those managing Japanese employees could also:

- Encourage the group as a whole. This inspires the strong to help or to compensate for the weak.
- Be ambiguous. Criticize in general, not specific, terms.
- Stress the desired result.

One more comment about criticism: If a Japanese complains about a husband or wife, it's likely just a form of self-effacement. If problems really did exist, they probably wouldn't bring them up.

Speeches

Even when introduced by name, a Japanese will usually begin a speech with, "As kindly introduced by Mr. So-and-so, I am Such-and-such." He will then often offer some words of gratitude or humility. He will not start off with "a funny thing happened to me on the way here" type of joke. Speeches are serious matters. They're usually designed to lend proper dignity to the occasion, not to entertain. People who joke too much, or too soon, are viewed as taking the subject at hand too lightly.

8
The Nonverbal Statement

No matter the country, what's communicated nonverbally says at least as much as what's communicated verbally. Posture, gesture, facial expression, silence, voice quality, proxemics (interpersonal distance), and dress all convey a message of some kind.

Because nonverbal cues and responses have a built-in ambiguity, they are less likely to create embarrassment or loss of face than those indicated directly and therefore are commonly used in Japan as a means of communication. As a Westerner, the more you understand these nonverbal cues, the greater your potential for discerning what the Japanese are really "saying."

The Role of Silence

In Japan silence is a virtue. Many Japanese proverbs proclaim the virtues of silence, a common one being, "Those who know do not speak. Those who speak do not know." In a television commercial, the macho movie star Toshirō Mifune admonishes: "Men, keep quiet, and drink Sapporo beer!"

It is during silent "meaningful intervals" that the famous belly language (*haragei*), the sensing of another's thoughts and feelings, goes on. The "gut-level feeling" they're trying to get may be of your sincerity or trustworthiness. They could also be trying to get a feeling of their colleagues' reactions to your proposal. In the first case, by breaking the silence you may appear to be trying to cover up your lack of sincerity. In the second, you would be getting in the way of them reaching an informal consensus and inadvertently contributing to the length of the discussions.

Breaking the silence has two additional drawbacks: (1) it makes us do most of the talking (and when you're talking, you're giving away information) and (2) it tends to make us offer concessions when it's not necessary.

It's not uncommon for Japanese to sit for many minutes without comment. Your best strategy is to learn to be comfortable with silence. Use the time to feel the other party out intuitively, to get closer by "resonating" with them. Try to figure out what they're thinking by getting their "vibes." Reflect on what has been discussed up to that point and plan your next move or question.

Understandably, being too quick to interpret a silent spell can get you into trouble. Besides being a time of "feeling out," silence could indicate a range of things—from comfort to discomfort, from disagreement to pure lack of understanding. If you are reasonably sure they've understood you, relax, be patient, and be quiet.

Facial Expressions

The poker face: The classic stoic expression so often seen in Japan is a remnant of the samurai days, when emotional turmoil was never to be displayed on the face. These days it serves as a buffer, like an invisible protective shield, in a crowded land where physical privacy is hard to come by. It is, of course, used to cover negative emotions as well, since suppression of feelings is still thought to be a virtue.

The smile: Like people everywhere, the Japanese smile and laugh at times of joy. There may be times, however, when you think, "What's so funny?" There may be nothing funny at all. In fact, something tragic may have just happened. The smile conceals the true anguish or embarrassment of the Japanese and attempts to spare you any sympathetic pain.

Indeed, anytime you hear a nervous laugh or see a smile that you think doesn't belong, it's almost certainly covering some sort of discomfort. At this time, it's best not to push the subject any further. On the other hand, a smile could be concealing some other feeling unknown to you. Until you know the person well, you're safer to avoid reading anything into it.

Eye contact: Through extensive reviews of video tapes of Japanese and American meetings, John Graham, of the University of California, Irvine, has found that Americans maintain approximately three times as much eye contact as Japanese do. In the West we're taught to look people in the eyes at all times; averting the eyes often signifies a lack of sincerity or confidence. In Japan, however, constant eye contact with a superior is considered rude. It may be seen as defiance or a challenge. So if at first a Japanese seems to be "shifty-eyed," he may simply be showing you respect.

Proxemics and Dynamics

When speaking to one another, the Japanese put more space between themselves than do Westerners, especially in formal situations. If you trespass into this personal territory, you will make your Japanese counterpart feel very uncomfortable. Resist the urge to take a step closer if your Japanese counterpart has taken a step back.

Americans like to enter a room and make heads turn. Someone who walks into a room with panache or an air of control of their surroundings makes an impression. In Japan, however, people are more sensitive to fitting in and will often try to make themselves smaller than life by being reserved and using humble speech.

A Japanese conforming to a situation in order to maintain harmony could be seen by Westerners as compromising. Conversely, someone whom Westerners would call "dynamic" might be seen by Japanese as overwhelming or pushy. A person whose energy is controlled or "centered" is respected in Japan. It's the subtlety of inner control and sensitivity toward others that makes the favorable impression.

Touching

Touching fellow workers and associates is not common in Japan. Patting on the back or putting a friendly arm around someone is not done. While there is some touching among close friends and people with whom one spends a lot of time, it's not something you can presume is welcome, so it's best not to initiate it. (A common exception, however, is when getting drunk together.)

Gestures

Every culture has its own set of gestures and hand signals. As members of an implicit, nonconfrontational society, Japanese tend to use small hand gestures, especially when referring to something negative, more frequently than people from many other cultures.

Some Japanese gestures will be familiar in appearance, but have a new set of meanings, so be careful. Because there are appropriate and inappropriate times to utilize these gestures (depending on the formality of the situation) it's advisable not to use them yourself. You do, however, want to be able to interpret the gestures when you see them.

A *negative* is indicated by fanning the right hand in front of the face as if waving away flies.

Nodding usually goes on constantly during a conversation to let the speaker know he is being *listened to* and *understood*.

Oneself, or *me,* is indicated by pointing to one's own nose (when Westerners would point to their chests). This gesture may be used in formal as well as informal situations.

Money is represented by forming a circle with the index finger and thumb, similar to our "okay" sign.

A *man* can be symbolized by our "thumbs up" sign. Depending on the context it could refer to a woman's lover, a father, or the president of a company.

A *woman* can be symbolized by sticking up the pinkie finger. Depending on the context it could refer to a man's lover.

Discomfort about what is being discussed or considered is expressed by placement of the hand on the back of one's neck.

Eating is mimed by holding an imaginary bowl in the left hand and making a motion with the right as if shoveling rice into the mouth with chopsticks.

To suggest *going drinking,* lifting a sake cup is mimicked with the index finger and thumb.

Beckoning someone to you is done European-style, similar to the way Americans wave good-bye, with the palm facing downward.

"Excuse me," used at such times as when walking between or in front of people, or when taking something being offered, is indicated by moving the hand repeatedly in front of the face as if slicing the air away from you.

Embarrassment (or appropriate *shyness* or *modesty*) is shown by women by covering the mouth.

If you make a fist next to your head (level with your ear) and release the fist all of a sudden, it indicates you think that someone is *crazy*.

Anger or *jealousy* is symbolized by pointing the index fingers up or angling them out from the temples.

Strained relations or *a fight* is shown by criss-crossing the index fingers or by tapping the index fingers together.

Belief that someone is *lying* can be symbolized by licking the index finger and smoothing an eyebrow.

In Japan, gestures in general are not as overt or as large as in the West. The axis of movement is more likely to be at the wrist than at the elbow or shoulder. It is thought that a mature person should have a subdued style. Likewise, any display of anger, disappointment, or frustration is considered childish.

One American gesture that does not have a particular meaning in Japan is an extended middle finger. A bilingual friend of mine was in a meeting with several Japanese and American executives. When she asked one of the Japanese where his next meeting was, he used his middle finger to point up to the next floor. The looks on the faces of the Americans, who hadn't understood the question, were priceless.

Voice, Dress, and Other Nonverbal Statements

There are several behaviors that you, as a Westerner, may have to curb in order to avoid making undesirable statements about yourself. First of all, try to keep your voice down, as speaking loudly is considered rude and threatening.

In addition to people, it's wise to show respect for objects, such as materials and reports presented to you. Try not to crumple up gift wrapping or any other type of paper before you throw it away. Do not fold or fiddle with business cards. Do not lean back in your chair or sit on furniture that is not meant for sitting on, such as a table or desk. Also do not take off your jacket or loosen your tie unless your counterpart does.

Remember that formality and respect are valued and that informality can be interpreted as disrespect.

In Japan, adults rarely wear bright colors or bold designs. Americans are often thought to be too casual or sloppy in their attire. You don't want to send the wrong message in a business interaction. Dress conservatively. For men, this means a blue, gray, or brown suit, and a tie that is not too bold. The peacock revolution has not yet reached Japan. After hours, things may be different, especially if you are socializing with younger people.

Women tend to wear livelier colors these days. However, if you wish to look more mature and consequently be taken more seriously, I recommend a conservative suit, both in color and in cut. Longer, fuller skirts are a real plus if you sit on *tatami* mats. Short skirts get *real* short when you sit on the floor!

Japanese, especially those who live in Tokyo, are very clothes conscious. They spend small fortunes on high-quality garments. Since this is one way of sizing people up, make sure yours are not communicating a lack of sophistication or prosperity. Even beginners, for example, have the latest tennis and ski attire.

Cologne and perfume are not traditionally used; yours could easily be overpowering. In Japan as in the West, chewing gum while speaking, is not to be done. Do not snap your fingers at a waiter or waitress (see chapter 11 for expressions to get someone's attention).

The Japanese are not a demonstrative people. While some younger couples may hold hands, the Japanese you will be dealing with in business will probably feel very uncomfortable if you, say, kiss your spouse, even in greeting.

Understanding the Japanese language is of major importance. However, without an understanding of the nonverbals, knowledge of the language could be useless. In Japan, it's everything they *didn't* say that is likely to be crucial. Try to be perceptive and, above all, don't presume you understand an act or behavior until you're absolutely sure of the meaning.

9
Tips for Cross-Cultural Communication

Communicating with someone from another culture can be a challenge. English spoken with a strong accent can sound like a foreign tongue. What's more, trying to figure out whether or not you have been understood correctly can be even more perplexing. Yet communication is an essential part of your relationship. Miscommunication can create business as well as social disasters.

Here are some simple ways to improve understanding, and your relationship, through good communication skills.

Slow Down

The most common complaint I hear from Japanese friends and counterparts is that we speak too quickly. For a Japanese person, trying to understand specialized terminology as well as subtle nuances in English can be very frustrating, especially when the speaker is in high gear. To make sure you're not going faster than your listeners can easily handle, pace yourself to their speaking speed. Try to use short, concise sentences.

Slowing down will allow you to choose words that add clarity to your thoughts and to articulate these words fully. This does not mean resorting to pigeon English. Speaking in distorted or incorrect English can easily be interpreted as patronizing.

Speaking more loudly will *not* help the other person understand you. Nothing is more pointless than someone yelling their comments to another person who doesn't understand.

Isolate Each Question

Avoid using double questions. For example, the query, "Do you want to end early or work until we've finished?" actually contains two questions. People hearing questions like this in a foreign language tend to only retain the second question and answer it. Give your listener a chance to answer one question before asking another, or say, "We can quit now or work until we've done. Which would you like to do?"

Use Open-Ended Questions

Open-ended questions are so named because they open the conversation up for more information by precluding a simple yes or no answer. These questions begin with what, who, how, when, and where. Rather than asking, "Do you think it will be done by the end of the month?" the question "When do you think it will be done?" is more apt to provide you with an honest opinion. As asking "why" can put a person on the defensive, use this interrogative carefully. Not only do open-ended questions provide you with more information than close-ended questions, but the answers will frequently allow you to determine whether the person is understanding you or not.

Take Turns Talking

There are fewer conversational overlays when Japanese speak to each other than when two Americans are speaking. In fact, Japanese often pause a couple of seconds after the other party is finished before offering a contribution. This shows respect for the speaker and consideration for what was said. The pause is often longer than Americans are used to so we typically pick up the trail of the conversation to keep it moving.

Because of this tendency, you need to make sure that you are not monopolizing the conversation. Remember that Japanese usually won't butt in, so it's advisable to make sure there is a balance. In a group you may want to wait several seconds after someone has finished to see if anyone besides yourself would like to speak.

Write Down Large Numbers

In the West large numbers are divided into units of thousands and then millions, but the Japanese have an additional unit for ten thousand called *man*. Therefore, when saying the number 856,932, for example, the Japanese would say "eighty-five *man* six thousand nine hundred thirty-two. The first word is "eighty" instead of "eight hundred." When large numbers are being tossed around, even experienced interpreters can make mistakes based on this difference. And losing a single digit can, of course, mean a lot of money. To complicate the matter further, a billion means 1,000,000,000 in the United States and 1,000,000,000,000 in Britain. Writing down the number alleviates these problems. Another unit you might find useful is *oku*, which equals 100 million. Ten *oku* equals a billion (or a thousand million in England).

Give Supportive Feedback

Protocol in Japan dictates that the listener constantly furnish positive interjections. This small form of encouragement can go a long way to help the person you're talking to feel confident and comfortable. The more you nod your head and say, "I see" and "really," the more you will appear to be a polite listener and the more forthcoming an infrequent speaker of English is likely to be.

Check and Clarify

Use active listening. This is the process of summarizing what you understood the other person to have said in order to verify your understanding. To do this well you must give your full attention to what is being said and be sure that when you are summarizing you attach no judgment or advice. This is an excellent way to make sure accurate communication has taken place, even when speaking to another English speaker. This process requires extra time, but what you'll gain in accuracy will be well worth it. It's a good idea to build time for verification into your meeting schedules.

Active listening is not something the Japanese are accustomed to doing so you should begin by modeling the technique yourself. When speaking on the phone or communicating technical information, accurate understanding becomes even more critical. You may want to agree ahead of time to use this as a checking device.

Don't forget to explain major points in two different ways. Because you can't be sure it was understood correctly when expressed in only one way, it's always safest to express an important factor from another angle. When communicating across cultures, making assumptions of any kind, including assuming the other party has understood, can be very dangerous.

Avoid Using Slang

Even Japanese who have studied English for some time may not have a good knowledge of our idioms, sayings, or slang. The trouble is that unless the listener is familiar with a particular expression, he may assume he understands your meaning because he is familiar with the words. Such literal interpretations can range from humorous to disastrous. A Japanese who speaks English fairly well may ask how money is exchanged when you "buy into an idea." I've been told of a negotiation between an American and a Japanese that took six months to gain momentum. When the American used the idiom, "That's a no-brainer," the Japanese took it personally and cut off the negotiation. Being told he had no brains was just too much for the Japanese negotiator. Only by making concessions was the American able to get the Japanese back to the bargaining table.

IDIOMS THAT MAY BE TAKEN LITERALLY

Piece of cake	Now you're talking
No-brainer	Ace in the hole
Get the ball rolling	Strike out
Buy into it	Cut-and-dried
Blank check	Out of this world
Put our heads together	Put my cards on the table
Hammer it out	Eye-opener
Get to first base	Bail out
Make cuts across the board	Bottom line
Ahead of the game	Up his sleeve
Carry out	Hit the nail on the head
We have come a long way	Hit the road
On top of it	Highway robbery
Run into problems	Have a ball
Beat around the bush	Get away with murder
There was a foul-up	Burn the midnight oil
Hard sell	Zero in on the problem
He's on the ball	We've got our backs against the wall

Use Jokes Cautiously

The Japanese will not take you seriously if you exhibit less than serious behavior during formal hours, such as telling jokes during a meeting. The Japanese have a strong sense of protocol and formality that dictates that there is a time and place for everything. Formal situations, including work, are not the place for joking around, which could make you appear immature and not serious.

Even during informal times it's best to take care in the use of jokes. I don't mean to say that the Japanese don't like to have fun or joke around. They are very fond of having fun, and being able to have fun together greatly speeds the bonding process. However, standard jokes are usually based on certain assumptions that don't necessarily exist in other cultures. Besides, if you are using an inter-preter, he or she is likely to say simply that you have "just told a joke," so "all please laugh, NOW!"

Keep in mind too that Japanese rarely use sarcasm, which could have a very negative effect. What you say may be taken at face value. If you sarcastically say, "That's great!" they may think that's your opinion. Such a misunderstanding could add to the damage if a problem is serious.

Avoid Negative Questions

Care must also be taken when asking or answering a negative question. In English we answer yes if the answer is affirmative and no if it's negative. In Japanese, however, the yes or no response affirms whether the questioner is correct. Hence, a response to the question "Aren't you going?" by someone who is not would be "Yes" (meaning "Yes, I am not going").

The best solution to this confusing situation is to not ask a negative question. If you are asked one, be sure to answer with a complete sentence—not just "yes" or "no." Sometimes even open-ended questions will be answered first with a "yes." For example, "How long do you think this is going to take?" may be answered with "Yes. It will probably take about two months."

10
Interpreters

Very few Japanese who have not spent time out of Japan actually speak or understand English well, although they will have studied it for anywhere from two to ten years. This is because emphasis has been placed on reading and writing, and the language was taught by teachers who usually were not English speakers. Consequently, you may be misled into thinking someone understands more than he actually does. When in doubt, writing it down often helps.

But the wisest, and certainly the safest, strategy is to use an interpreter. Trying to do any serious negotiating in Japanese is a dangerous proposition. The circumlocutions and polite forms of the language make true understanding very elusive. Furthermore, once the subject of a sentence has been mentioned, it is rarely restated, even in the form of a pronoun.

Whether you are using a professional interpreter or a bilingual individual within the company you are visiting, you should take steps to ensure that you will be represented as accurately as possible. I once heard a very interesting speech in English make absolutely no sense in the Japanese translation, solely because one sentence was left out in the beginning. This wasn't because the translator was incompetent; on the contrary, he was quite capable. The problem was that too much was said in English before he was given an opportunity to put it into Japanese, and the translator apparently had not been briefed in advance on the main ideas of the talk.

Here is a list of ways to avoid such problems before they happen:

- Request a translator who is familiar with the specific field you're dealing in.
- Speak slowly and distinctly, without using slang, sports talk, obscure expressions, or superfluous words.
- Brief your translator ahead of time as thoroughly as possible. If you are giving a talk or presentation, give him a copy of it if you have one, and allow him time to question you or refer to a dictionary to clarify unclear terms in advance. If it is not a written talk, try to explain each major point in two different ways, and be sure one is free of idiom.
- Use short sentences, and don't go on at length without pausing for translation. Don't speak for more than two minutes without allowing for translation. What you say will be translated more accurately, and your listener won't have to wait so long before understanding what is being said.
- When speaking, look at your counterpart, not your interpreter.
- Listen to yourself as you speak and ask yourself if what you said was clear or if it could be taken in the wrong way. If so, make the same point again, putting it a different way.
- Do not interrupt your interpreter while he is speaking or listening.
- Avoid making assumptions of any kind.
- If your interpreter asks you many questions that seem unwarranted, get a new interpreter.

I highly recommend you retain your own interpreter as opposed to using someone from the Japanese side's company. You may be able to get valuable feedback from him or her about how things are coming across or what is required of you at a specific time. Be sure to take time to debrief afterward to get the interpreter's opinion on the Japanese team and what transpired. Off-the-record perceptions are difficult to convey during a meeting.

Older interpreters, while possibly not as fluent in English as some younger ones, can lend you credibility and respectability. However, remember that, whether young or old, your interpreter has an extremely difficult and stressful job. Allow for plenty of breaks and be understanding of mistakes. The Japanese hold impatient people in low esteem, so, above all, be patient. This will not only help things go smoothly but will make you look more professional.

Your *shōkai-sha*, your embassy, or your chamber of commerce in Japan may be able to recommend an interpreter or one may be hired through the organizations found in appendix C. Large hotels can also provide you with an interpreter for a fee.

Some Essential Expressions

Even if you never learn to speak Japanese, learning just a few critical phrases can make a large difference, both in convenience and in the way your Japanese counterparts view you. Though it's just a token gesture on your part, using these phrases signifies a certain respect for custom and courtesy.

Phonetics

Unlike English, Japanese is very phonetic, and pronunciation of new words is therefore quite predictable. Note that the pronunciation of a particular vowel or consonant does not vary at all from one word to the next.

Some vowels are held longer than others; this is usually indicated in transliterations by a ⁻ (long vowel) mark over it or by doubling the vowel. One must be careful here because an elongated vowel changes the meaning of the word. For example *ie* means "house," but *iie* means "no." Even in Japanese words we often use, some of the vowels should be held longer. For example, Tokyo, Osaka, and Kyoto are actually Tōkyō, Ōsaka, and Kyōto.

The most common English spellings of Japanese are from the Hepburn or Standard system, the transliteration used throughout this book.

Pronunciation is as follows:

A—"ah" as in father
E—"eh" as in set
I—"ee" as in machine
O—"oh" as in go
U—"oo" as in June

The Japanese "r" is something between the American "l," "r," and "d." It is slightly rolled by bouncing the tongue off the base of the upper teeth. This means the Japanese have a hard time distinguishing between our "r" and "l," in both hearing and pronouncing it. My last name, for example, ends up sounding something like "Rowrand" or "Lowland." Don't be offended by these mistakes. Our rendition of Japanese words is usually much worse.

A "singsongy" style can make it very difficult for the Japanese to understand you. Compared with English, Japanese is spoken with little modulation or inflection. While there is some variation in pitch, there is no emphasis on different syllables the way we stress accent syllables in English. Practice by saying HI-RO-SHI-MA without any variation in stress on the syllables, rather than HI-ro-SHI-ma as we normally say, or even Hi-RO-shi-ma as some who know a little Japanese do to try to compensate for an undesirable Western accent. The pitch does rise slightly, however, on the last three syllables.

A Necessary Vocabulary

Below is a short list of words that will come in handy for courtesy and convenience. The list has been pared down to include only those words that, if you know no others, will keep you from appearing utterly barbarian or that are useful because no equivalent exists in English. A hyphenated "o" preceding a word represents an honorific that may be dropped in less polite speech.

If you are planning to travel to Japan, take a few Japanese lessons before you go or at the very least get yourself a good phrase book (see appendix F).

Common Expressions

Dōzo means "please," as in "Please come in" or "Please go ahead," *not* as a request.

Onegai shimasu (informal: *onegai;* more formal: *onegai itashimasu*) means, in essence, "I make this request" or "I'm asking you this favor" or "please."

Yoroshiku means something like, "I hope for your continued friendship or goodwill." However,

Yoroshiku onegai shimasu is a request for a continued friendship and is usually said when first meeting people. It can also appropriately be said at the end of a negotiating session or at the end of a speech to people you hope to be doing business with.

Satō san ni yoroshiku. "Please give my regards to Mr. Satō."

Dōmo arigatō gozaimasu. "Thank you very much." *Dōmo* or *arigatō* can stand alone to convey thanks or can be combined, without *gozaimasu,* to mean thank you.

Arigatō gozaimasu can be used for a more polite thank-you. *Dōmo* by itself can also be used as a casual greeting. The past tense (*gozaimashita*) is used for an act that has been completed.

Dō itashimashite. "You're welcome."

Hai, wakarimasu. "Yes, I understand."

Iie, wakarimasen. "No, I don't understand."

Chotto matte kudasai. "Wait a minute, please" (used in informal situations).

Saah. "Hmmmm."

Ah sō desu ka. "Is that so?"

Ne. "Isn't it?" "You know?" (tacked on to the end of a sentence).

Introductions

Hajimemashite. "How do you do? It's my first time to have the pleasure."

(Global) no (Smith) desu. "I am (Smith) of (Global)."

Dōzo yoroshiku. "Please look upon this relationship favorably. Please feel kindly disposed toward me."

Greetings

Irasshaimase. "Welcome" (used mostly at stores and restaurants).

Yōkoso irasshaimashita. "Welcome" (informal: *yōkoso*).

Moshi moshi. "Hello" (telephone).

Itsumo osewa ni natte orimasu. "I am always in your debt" (that is, "Thank you for everything you do for me").

Ohayō gozaimasu. "Good morning (informal: *ohayō*).

Konnichiwa. "Good afternoon."

Konbanwa. "Good evening."

Oyasuminasai. "Good night."

Sayōnara. "Good-bye."

Expressions of Consideration

Sumimasen. "Excuse me" or "Thank you" (literally, "It is never-ending, my indebtedness to you"). Prefacing it with *dōmo* makes it more polite; the combined phrase can be used when receiving a gift. *Sumimasen* by itself can be used to get the attention of a waiter in a restaurant.

Mōshiwaki gozaimasen. One of the strongest ways to say, "I'm sorry."

Osaki ni is said when doing anything before somebody else, such as eating, leaving, or entering an elevator.

Ganbatte kudasai. "Hang in there" or "Do your best."

Otsukaresama deshita. "Thank you for your hard work" (for example, to someone who has been working hard all day and is staying late in the office).

Gokurōsama deshita. "Thank you for your trouble" (to someone who has done a favor for you; not said to superiors).

Odaiji ni. "Take good care of yourself" (to someone who is sick).

Dining

Itadakimasu literally means "I humbly receive." It is said to the host or hostess before starting a meal.

Go chisō sama. "It was a treat" ("Thank you for the meal"). (Adding *deshita* makes it more polite.)

Kanpai. "Cheers!"

Written Japanese

The Japanese language is a mixture of *kanji* (characters taken from Chinese) and two phonetic alphabets, *hiragana* and *katakana*. Traditionally a page is read from top to bottom, right to left. *Kanji* are symbols that represent meanings rather than sounds. They can be understood without knowing how to pronounce them.

Hiragana and *katakana* are two alphabets, or actually syllabaries, comprised of forty-six phonetic symbols each. *Hiragana* is used for such things as particles and verb endings. *Katakana*, used for foreign words, is very useful to know even if your stay in Japan will be short. For example, since many technical terms are borrowed from English and hence written in Japanese using *katakana*, the English terms they use may have a *katakana* pronunciation. Technical people will find it very easy to understand technical Japanese if they learn how to read *katakana*.

Survival *Kanji*

お手洗い	o-te arai	rest room
女	onna	female
男	otoko	male
入口	iriguchi	entrance

出口	deguchi	exit
駅	eki	station
北口	kita guchi	North exit
南口	minami guchi	South exit
東口	higashi guchi	East exit
西口	nishi guchi	West exit
郵便局	yūbinkyoku	post office
禁煙	kin'en	no smoking
銀行	ginkō	bank
東京	Tokyo	
京都	Kyoto	
大阪	Osaka	

Katakana

タクシー	takushii	taxi
バス	basu	bus

コーヒー	kōhii	coffee
ビール	biiru	beer
ホテル	hoteru	hotel

12
Correspondence

As with other things Japanese, many aspects of their written correspondence differ from the Western style. For starters, it usually takes much longer to get to the main point of the letter. Most conversations in the West go from the specific to the general, taking care of business before pleasantries are discussed. American correspondence, likewise, is usually to the point and specific at the beginning and becomes more general toward the end.

A Japanese letter, however, is just the reverse, proceeding first from the general to the specific. A personal letter will usually be handwritten and begin with a comment about the weather or the season. If you are writing in spring, it may be a remark about how beautiful the cherry blossoms are. "I hope you are staying cool during this very hot and humid weather" would be appropriate in mid-July and August; "The fall colors must be very brilliant in Japan right now," in October and November; and "You must be very busy with preparations for the New Year," when sending a letter in late December.

A Japanese letter ends with a closing phrase at the bottom, followed by the date toward the top of the next line. The date, too, is reversed from ours, giving first the year, then month, then the day. Next comes the name of the writer at the bottom of the next line. The receiver's name appears at the top of the last line, another show of respect toward the person to whom the letter is written.

拝啓

早春のみぎりいかがお過ごしでしょうか、お伺い申し上げます。

さて、昨年来、私の就職に際しまして、すっかりお世話になり、ありがとうございました。お陰様で入社手続きもすみ、あとは四月一日の入社式を待つばかりでございます。

入社後は、先日お伺い致しました教訓を守り、なるべく早く仕事に慣れ、頑張ろうと思っております。今後とも、何卒ご指導下さいますよう宜しくお願い致します。

まずは右、お礼申し上げます。

敬具

五十嵐 新太郎 様

平成四年三月十七日

山 田 太 郎

March 17, 1992

Dear Mr. Igarashi:

The season of early spring is here at last after such a long winter. I would like to inquire first how you have been faring?

In regards to my job search, I am so indebted to you and I want to thank you for all your help last year. Thanks to you, all the employment paperwork for my new job has been completed, and now the only thing left is to wait for the new employees' ceremony on April first.

After I begin working for the company I will remember the good advice you gave me when we spoke last. I will do my best to adapt to the new job as soon as possible, and I plan to work hard. Even then, I look forward to continuing to receive your guidance.

Words cannot adequately express my feelings, but for now please accept my gratitude as voiced above.

Sincerely yours,

Tarō Yamada

The Business Letter

Stylistically, business letters differ slightly from personal correspondence. For example, business letters may begin with such a phrase as "We are so happy that your business is becoming even more prosperous." As with other types of Japanese communication, when making an appeal in written form, demands are made in a "softer" manner and persuasion is more subtle than is common in the West. Business letters, as well as personal letters, almost always include some sort of reference to the relationship and the desire for its continuance.

As in the West, business letters are written horizontally. The vertical style is used more commonly in personal correspondence.

Faxes

In Japan, decisions are rarely made over the telephone. However, after a telephone conversation, you may wish to confirm by fax anything that has been decided, such as a meeting time or date. In this way, you keep communication strong and clear between both parties. You may even wish to confirm a fax by telephone.

There is no special protocol for sending faxes, although by their nature they are much less formal than a standard business letter. Remember that Japanese are usually not versed in colloquial English, so make sure your fax is written in simple and clear language, without sentences or words that can be taken in more than one way.

Which Style to Use?

If you are writing a letter in English, by all means use the standard American form. However, the following Japanese letter may give you insight into a style that is acceptable in Japan. Since it is personal in nature, this letter should ideally be handwritten to convey an added sense of personal attention.

III

NEGOTIATING

13
Business Values

In the game of Japanese business, many of the rules are unwritten, and figuring out what conventions apply at any given time is not easy. But understanding the business values that mold the conventions will give you a better sense of how to score—and how to avoid penalties.

Reciprocal Obligation

The concept of reciprocal obligation dictates that one must return favors, gifts, dinners, information, influence, introductions, and so on. This obligation can even be carried on from one generation to another, and the longer one waits the more one seems to owe, as if it collected interest. Obligations can become valuable commodities. Depending on who the other party is, just knowing that he "owes you one" can provide more peace of mind than a good insurance policy.

Corporations can also incur obligation. When dealing with a Japanese company, it's important to find out what sort of obligations it may have and if these will affect your proposal. If the company is indebted to your competitor, it may mean you don't have a chance. On the other hand, you might be able to compensate by finding out the competitor's weak points and highlighting these aspects of your product or service.

Continuity

The Japanese treasure continuity between people and corporations. This is one reason a Japanese person will usually bring up the last time he talked to the other party and thank him for the occasion, whether it was a dinner, a phone call, a letter, or whatever. He will send greeting cards and presents at the appropriate time. The Japanese value the history of a relationship. In fact, the quality and length of the past relationship is some indication of prospects for the future. For this reason it is beneficial to send personal, non-sales-pitch letters following a visit from either side. A photo album documenting the business hurdles and the informal bonding the relationship has gone through contributes to the sense of longevity.

Loyalty to Group

Loyalty to groups is highly encouraged in Japan. For individuals this means a loyalty to other group members, to the company, and, in the largest sense, to the country. For companies, this means a loyalty to other members of the corporate group they belong to. Sometimes Japanese decisions that seem irrational to the Westerner are based on loyalty to a relationship. And there are many old relationships in Japan.

Remember, too, that group loyalty and other influences encourage the Japanese concept of insider/outsider. Not only are there different commitments to insiders, but there are entirely different rules of behavior. In fact, it would be more accurate to say that most of the rules apply only to insiders and that rules governing behavior to outsiders are hazy at best.

As long as you are perceived as an outsider you may be subjected to gross inconsistencies that would not be experienced by someone who has forged a partnership with the Japanese. You may even find yourself being taken advantage of. The sooner you establish yourself as a partner and not an outsider, the better your chances of success.

There are many things you can do to diminish the impression of being an outsider. One is exhibiting behavior that makes Japanese feel comfortable. Learning some of their language and customs, for example, makes you seem much more one of the group. Learning about and following sumo or a local baseball team helps to break down barriers.

Possibly most important, though, is to avoid taking an adversarial position. By putting yourself in the adversarial role that Westerners often use, you will rarely increase your bargaining power. Instead you will be perceived as being hopelessly on the outside. The more you appear as an adversary, the more risky your position.

Saving Face and Peer Pressure

In Japan, self-respect is based in large part on others' opinions, so saving face becomes a critical issue. A company may continue to do business with another even when it is no longer profitable, so that the companies and the go-between will not lose face.

The purpose of protocol is to avoid an awkward or embarrassing situation. Embarrassment can cause a loss of face and consequently predictable, polite behavior is highly desirable.

Also, the more presence you have in Japan, the less likely the Japanese will be to behave in an unethical manner. Peer pressure is a strong motivator to behave respectably, and *everything* gets around in Japan.

Patience and Persistence

Japanese believe that patience and persistence will eventually pay off. They're not as conditioned into thinking that success comes from "getting a break." They believe in persisting, in hanging in, something they call *ganbaru*. Having the *ganbaru* spirit is an important quality in a person, one you'll definitely need if you want to succeed in Japan.

14
Negotiating Using Japanese Ground Rules

When at last you sit down at the bargaining table with the Japanese, you may find that the negotiating process differs from what you're used to. Gearing your expectations to match what is likely to happen will minimize your frustrations later on.

For starters, be prepared to commit an extra measure of patience and people. Here's why:

- Every stage of the negotiating process will take appreciably longer than you are accustomed to.
- You won't know exactly where you stand until the contract is signed.
- The Japanese team will try to outnumber you whenever possible.

Time to Get Acquainted

When setting up business connections, the Japanese businessman's first concern is to develop a friendly and trusting relationship. This takes time. At this early stage, there may even be several meetings, lunches, dinners and drinking nights at which no business is discussed at all. Don't try to rush things or get things moving. Let your Japanese counterparts initiate the business discussion, unless it was they who approached you for the transaction at hand. The one being pursued, of course, has the upper hand, and can take more initiative.

Since relationships in Japan are conceived of as ideally long-term, they carry with them a great deal of personal obligation and are entered into consciously and cautiously. The Japanese will make sure that new business relationships evolve according to customary rituals. To them, the established friendships and harmonious atmosphere of these initial meetings are more important for the moment than the potential terms of the business deal. The stage that you set now can have a great effect on how negotiations go later.

Decision by Group

The Japanese practice of sharing the responsibility for decision making is another reason why the negotiating process takes so long. Although some companies are headed by founder-presidents who have total decision-making authority, the traditional sharing of the decision-making process is much more common.

A business proposal is usually initiated within a Japanese company at the middle or lower levels of management. It takes the form of a *ringi-sho*, a written proposal that is circulated laterally and then upward. Each person who sees it affixes his personal seal of approval.

This process is called *ringi-seido* (request for decision system). It emphasizes the importance the Japanese place on group decisions. It also takes a lot of time. This is mainly because a great deal of informal discussion will have taken place before the *ringi-sho* is even drawn up.

In negotiations this system means you will have to win the confidence of the entire group, not just one person. Although it may be frustrating to have to establish personal relationships with all the decision makers, in the long run it will be worth the effort. Learn to use the system; get input from all people involved, and revise your proposal to meet their concerns as much as possible. This may seem terribly time-consuming and tedious, but in the end it is much more productive than idly waiting for a long-delayed response, especially when that response may be merely a request for more information.

If what you are proposing is a major deal involving substantial up-front cash or credit, then lower-level management or even reasonably high-up managers may not want to risk their reputations or positions. In this case you may need to use outside connections or government pressure through the Ministry of International Trade and Industry (MITI) or Japan External Trade Organizations (JETRO; see appendix C) to influence the highest-level decision makers.

Letting Negotiations Evolve

Especially in preliminary meetings when each side is gathering subtle clues as to where the other side stands, it's wise to be humble, indirect, good-natured, and, most of all, nonthreatening. Suppress any inclination to take charge and get things moving.

Do not simply lay your cards on the table. Play them one at a time. The Japanese may doubt your integrity if you make concessions too soon. Compromises and concessions are usually made at the end of all discussions, as opposed to the Western style of negotiating terms one by one. If you can, let your Japanese counterparts initiate the concessions.

When agreements are reached, go over each point to make sure both sides are agreeing to the same thing. When it is necessary to disagree on something, do so in a disguised fashion.

Learn how to be agreeable without agreeing and how to disagree without being disagreeable. Say "Basically I agree with you, but I must discuss it with my seniors" or "I agree with what you have said for the most part, but I have a few small questions." You may often hear the former phrase in Japan, since the people you'll be dealing with probably do not have authority to make final decisions. Generally speaking, the Japanese desire a decision or agreement in which there is no obvious winner and loser.

Showing your Japanese counterparts copies of faxes and other correspondence with your home office demonstrates your sincerity and respect for them as "partners" in the negotiations. Of course, use discretion and do not share classified or sensitive information with anyone.

One difficulty in dealing with Japanese who have had previous experience with Americans is that they may come to the table with preconceived ideas of what tactics are necessary. If their past experiences have been with argumentative and confrontational Americans, they may try to incorporate these features into their strategy. The danger of this is that since it is not typical in their culture, they have no gauge to tell them what is too much. I have seen Japanese behave in an uncharacteristically aggressive manner when dealing with Americans, to the degree that a normally humble person suddenly acquired an arrogant, intimidating style.

This is a tricky situation for you. Responding in kind will reinforce their perception that this is appropriate behavior. It is probably safer to encourage them to take a more Japanese approach by being as cooperative as possible and not being confrontational.

A common method of avoiding confrontation is to employ the services of a go-between (*chūkai-sha*). You can be as frank and direct as you wish with a go-between without risking injury to the other party. Only direct confrontation results in loss of face.

Help the group to reach a consensus. Make changes and provide support materials and data as necessary to enable your supporters to persuade others. Cover all your bases by asking each individual involved how to establish a good relationship with the others. Make sure that you do not create threatening or embarrassing situations that will interfere with a harmonious consensus in your favor. In the end, the decision can be implemented quickly and with full cooperation when it already has unanimous support.

If a major stumbling block is encountered during negotiations, it could well last for several weeks. You have little recourse other than to keep the channels open, especially at the lower levels. A mutual friend or go-between may be able to find out what the problem is and possibly influence things a little; if not, be as patient as you can be. The best thing to do is simply to set your watch and your expectations on Japanese time. Be flexible. And even if things seem pleasant, don't assume that all is well.

15
The Negotiating Team

In the West there is a propensity for "going it alone." A certain amount of prestige is associated with negotiating a good contract single-handedly. This Superman complex, however, can put you at a great disadvantage in negotiations with the Japanese.

The Japanese negotiating team is likely to include an interpreter, the chief executive officer (present only during formalities), middle managers to sanction decisions, operational staff to work out the details, and possibly financial and technical experts as well. In addition, there will usually be someone whose main responsibilities are to listen, to watch for nonverbal clues, and to run errands.

A single Westerner cannot adequately fill all these roles.

Assistants not only add prestige to your team, they complement the Japanese operational staff who are the real negotiators on the other team. More important, the most valuable channels of communication between the two negotiating teams are informal ones between the lower-level members of each. When problems arise that would be thought to disrupt harmony if revealed at higher levels, they can often be resolved in explicit conversation between these lower-level members over an after-work drink. The real truth—*honne*—can then be shared. It's critical that a trusting relationship be established at this level early on.

The Japanese are sometimes resentful when a foreign company sends a young businessman as a representative. To them it indicates that the company places little importance on negotiations. To their way of thinking, age and seniority command respect. Indeed, promotion and salary are usually based on length of service with the Japanese company. On the other hand, a high-ranking official taking part in informal negotiations makes them feel undue pressure. It is also considered rude. A combination of middle- and lower-management representatives is best.

It is also an excellent idea to have someone just to watch and listen. This observer can, for example, count the number of times the other side brings up a subject—a good indicator of priorities.

If you are negotiating on your own territory, you can usually find out ahead of time the number and positions of those who are coming; organize your team accordingly. Almost certainly, the Japanese will be calculating the same for a team of Westerners visiting them. Even if you show up in Japan with more team members than they expected, they will try to add people at the last minute, making sure they match or exceed your number to give themselves the edge.

How to Choose Your Team

Colleen Kelley and Judith Meyers, developers of the Cross-Cultural Adaptability Inventory, have done an extensive study of published research in the area of cross-cultural effectiveness (appendix C for how to obtain their self-assessment questionnaire). They have concluded that there are four skill areas that are most useful to people working internationally. These skills include:

1. The ability to keep a positive attitude while dealing effectively with such difficult emotions as frustration, depression, and anxiety.
2. The ability to be open-minded about different types of people and ways of thinking.
3. The ability to perceive and respond to verbal and nonverbal communication cues.
4. The ability to maintain a sense of values and personal identity independent of the situation.

If members of your team are deficient in any of these areas you may want to consider obtaining some general cross-cultural training in addition to training in dealing with the Japanese culture.

When you are in the process of selecting your team, remember that the Japanese are most kindly disposed toward people who are quiet, warm-hearted, friendly, and willing to compromise, and who are good at listening (the importance of this skill can't be overemphasized). Many Japanese are uncomfortable with very extroverted people. Extroverts are often regarded as too up-front and superficial. Others cannot get a feel for them because they are "on" all the time and seem to be wearing a mask to hide their true selves. Introverted people are more introspective, more in sync with the Japanese character. This bit of reserve will make you appear more mature and wise. Japanese are also uncomfortable with people who are loud, aggressive, unpredictable, uncompromising, insensitive, and patronizing.

Those who have influence at your company headquarters are important team members as they will usually be the ones who will have to sell the final proposal to decision makers back home. Above all, choose people who know how to rely on and get along with the other members of the team.

The Role of Lawyers

As members of a litigious society, Americans like to take precautionary legal measures when they enter into a business deal. We base our business interaction on fulfilling performance clauses in contracts. In Japan, however, the business interaction is based on how the relationship is built and maintained, not what you've managed to inject into a contract. Situations or conditions may change. In the Japanese view, the partners must adapt to new circumstances and modify an agreement in an appropriate manner. You can see the problem then in having your lawyer at the negotiating table. It's difficult to develop a good relationship when you have someone present whose role appears to be to trap the other side.

As Japanese business has become more international, their attitude toward consulting attorneys during negotiations has changed significantly. The advantage of having a clearly worded understanding between two parties whose expectations may be very different is becoming apparent to many. Multinational Japanese companies have long retained foreign lawyers. But now even individuals and small companies who did not get what they thought had been agreed to in their American deals are often seeking counsel. Some are learning that there are Americans who won't honor an agreement unless it's enforced.

The key to making this situation work for both sides is sensing at what point you can bring your attorney in without inciting mistrust from the other side. For large Japanese companies that have been dealing internationally for some time, this point will be much earlier than for a small domestic company on an outer island. It will also greatly help the situation if your counsel knows how to project the image that he or she is ultimately concerned with the welfare and satisfaction of both parties involved.

Present a United Front

It is critical to your success that your team presents an undivided position. Disagreeing among yourselves in front of the Japanese team will convey weakness and lack of preparation. Develop team signals for taking a break to discuss controversial opinions. The Japanese, of course, have the advantage of being able to hold a discussion in front of most foreign teams without them understanding the details of the conversation. To be able to accomplish the same task you will need to take a break or develop a coded set of gestures or language. (I've used pig Latin with success.)

The problem will greatly be diminished if you take time to fully brief your team members and listen to the concerns they might have in advance. Not doing this will decrease your effectiveness as a team and increase your chance for wasting time during an exceedingly expensive trip to Japan. If your team members are coming from different locations, I recommend meeting in Hawaii before proceeding on to Tokyo. Besides giving you the opportunity to get your act together, it will help ease the jet lag when you arrive in Japan.

16
What About Women?

The traditional role for women in Japan, as elsewhere in the world, has been in the home. While seemingly subservient in public, a woman wields much power in her own domain. Not only is the education of children entirely in her hands, but she also controls the purse strings. She makes virtually all the purchasing decisions and gives her husband pocket money, often limiting it to an amount she deems appropriate.

Tradition dictates that it is the mother's responsibility to bring out the children's best qualities and to motivate them to work hard so they will have a successful life. Women take this role very seriously. The notorious "education mama" has been known to take it to an extreme, such as sitting in on her child's after-school cram classes to take notes if he or she is sick.

Because of overtime and after-work activities the husband does not usually play an active part in raising the children. In fact, a common saying among Japanese women is, "The best husband is healthy and absent." Younger women, however, are demanding that their husbands take a more active role not only in child-rearing, but also as a helper with household chores and as a companion.

The Office Lady

Most companies hire young women, called office ladies (or O.L.s), to make tea and do general office work. It's commonly assumed they will quit and get married in their mid-twenties, and thus they are not regarded as lifetime employees. Career women have been a rarity. (This is changing in ways that are discussed in chapter 27.)

The Western Businesswoman

The bad news is that Japanese men who have not been abroad are not used to dealing with women as equals in a business setting. They are not, however, used to dealing with foreigners either. Although many Japanese are uncomfortable with either, it is primarily due to a lack of experience. The good news is that being a foreign female is not a double disadvantage. In fact, after the initial awkwardness, I've often seen it to be an advantage. Being a novelty, for example, is an asset right off the bat.

Foreign women can also seem less intimidating to the Japanese than foreign men, especially large, aggressive men. Women are often seen as more culturally sensitive, and you can amplify this advantage by becoming more knowledgeable than other foreigners about Japanese language and culture. You may then find yourself being asked to take control in intercultural encounters when someone at your level would not normally be asked to assume such a role. Develop whatever assets you have that others around you may not have or use.

If you are a Western woman doing business with the Japanese, it is essential that you view how you are treated with open-mindedness and sensitivity. Taking an aggressive, indignant stand against time-honored traditions will get you nowhere. In time, the people you are working with will accept you for who and what you are. Skills and ability are recognized and valued whether you are male or female, but it may require an extra dose of diligence to prove yourself.

Even after your Japanese colleagues become accustomed to your professional contribution, they could be less comfortable with you in social situations. Keep in mind that Japanese men have little experience in socializing with women on an equal business level; the women they've dealt with in business have usually been in subservient roles. They will have a harder time relating to you if you seem very extroverted, overconfident, or aggressive.

If you are meeting Japanese associates with a Western male colleague, the Japanese will probably initially form a sense of group identity with him and direct most of the conversation his way (he's part of the "male group"). However, there are other group identities that may take precedence, such as "company" or "acquaintance." There have been many occasions when Japanese counterparts would direct their conversation toward me rather than my American male colleagues. Perhaps because of my experience in Japan they felt more of an affinity with me than with men who seemed "foreign."

The point here is that a businesswoman will probably be most effective if she can appear in some way sympathetic to matters Japanese. This will help to disabuse the Japanese of their stereotype of the Western woman as presumptuous and self-righteous.

Make sure your Japanese counterparts understand your status as early as possible, otherwise they are likely to assume you are playing a supportive role. Try to have a male colleague introduce you with your qualifications. Make it a point to repeat your name and title when you are being introduced. Sell your particular assets without tooting your own horn. If you are the main presenter, it would be useful to have someone of a lower or even equal level set things up and introduce you.

As elsewhere, credibility may be a little harder to come by for a woman, so make sure you know all the details about every relevant issue you can. Your Japanese counterparts may want to know details about your manufacturing locations or even the population of your state, county, or city.

Western businesswomen have already adapted to an environment and system not created by them, so make use of that skill and extend it to your relationships with your Japanese counterparts. You may be more diplomatic than your male colleagues. If this is true, use it to your advantage in the negotiation process.

It will also help you to be sensitive to some of the Japanese priorities that may differ markedly from your own. They may be horrified, for example, if a pregnant woman takes a business trip.

There are a wide variety of companies. Some still harbor traditional prejudices while others are more progressive. Be prepared to adapt to each new situation. Be forewarned that as a woman you will have to work harder and be more dedicated and flexible. But, if you succeed in cementing good relationships, the rewards may far outweigh your efforts and surpass what you could accomplish in your own country.

17
Meeting Etiquette

When negotiating with the Japanese, your interaction will certainly involve numerous meetings. Not only will the meeting etiquette differ somewhat from that in the West, but you may find that the goal of the meetings deviates from your expectations. Japanese meetings tend to serve one of three main purposes: to build or maintain rapport, to exchange information, or to confirm a decision that has already been reached informally. Rarely is the intention to reach a decision then and there.

During initial meetings, Japanese will try to get a feeling about the other party and establish a foundation of good communication based on trust and shared goals. It will help to create a good impression if you have some knowledge of the etiquette, but this concern should not get in the way of your ability to appear genuine and sincere.

Start things off right by being punctual. Getting across Tokyo can take hours, so be prepared for that. When people have very busy schedules, some exception is made for the difficulties of a commute between two meeting locations, but don't let this be the way your relationship begins. (Getting around in Tokyo is actually faster by bicycle, making this the favored means of transferring billions of dollars from bank to bank every day.)

Japanese meetings tend to have more ceremonial aspects than meetings in the West. During the initial meeting this will probably entail providing a spoken discourse on your company's history. Be prepared for this even if you know they already know your corporate chronicle. (Chances are they will know it better than you do.) This is a ritual that emerges from the Japanese pride in their past. It also gives them a chance to get a feel for your personal knowledge and style, as well as a sense of your true corporate goals.

Luncheon meetings are rare in Japan; lunch breaks are rather short affairs. Many Japanese eat at their desks or grab a quick bite close by. If you do go to lunch with them, don't expect business discussions to continue. Alcohol is almost never consumed during lunchtime.

Seating by Rank

If you are unclear about the level of the people you are meeting, pay close attention to the order in which they are introduced: The highest will be first. At meetings or restaurants people also enter and are seated in that order. In meetings, the top people will be in the middle of the table with descending ranks to their sides. The guests will be seated facing the door. As a guest it is polite to wait to be directed to your seat.

Specific roles or topics to be handled by individuals are predetermined based on their expertise. The top person present will lead the general discussion, turning over different topics to people on his right and left who also may call upon others with more detailed knowledge. After handing over the meeting to one of his subordinates, a high-ranking person may not participate much further as his role is primarily ceremonial. Be careful not to embarrass this person by asking him detailed questions he is not likely to know. Lower-level personnel handle the substance of a project.

Japanese meetings are characterized by a large amount of written material, which is distributed to each person present. One of the most common mistakes foreigners make is not bringing enough of their material with them to Japan. Two or three brochures written in English are not adequate for a team of several members. What may seem to be too much can easily turn out to be not enough. Always bring a surplus of everything.

Meetings open and close with such formalities as bows and

MEETING SEATING PROTOCOL

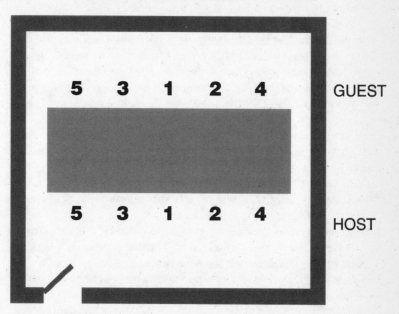

ceremonious words. Green tea, the national drink, is usually served early on (milk and sugar *never* go in green tea) and may be followed later with coffee or a soft drink. Even after the drink is put before you, you should wait until they invite you to drink (in Japanese, the word is *dōzo*). Even if you don't like green tea it is important that you drink some, as business discussions will usually not resume until the guest has had at least a sip.

Since early meetings serve to establish the relationship, questions and conversation tend to be quite general in nature. As the meetings proceed, it will be necessary to gather and exchange a great deal of information. Japanese will want to examine every detail possible before a decision is even considered. They will request copious amounts of information, some of it seemingly unrelated. This allows them to get a big picture as soon as possible and understand the context of the proposal. There is no reason, however, that all the information should flow in one direction. Be prepared with your questions and try to keep some degree of reciprocity in the exchange.

Japanese may ask you the same question more than once. It is essential to their credibility that every detail be meticulously covered at this stage. Should things not go well later, they would be embarrassed and possibly lose face if they had not done their job well. It could also be that they are checking your consistency or that you've hit upon an area where they have little flexibility.

Very often, however, they are prompted by a desire to decipher your true motivations. If you listen carefully you may discover they have asked the same question in a slightly different way that will provide them with slightly different information. Since asking the same question more than once is not considered rude in Japan, you should by all means take advantage of this technique to understand as much about them as possible.

Remember that a meeting is not the place or the time to put someone on the spot. A showdown will probably cause someone to lose face. Keep in mind the Japanese practice of group identity and speak accordingly. Don't single people out with either negative or positive attention.

It can be very useful for you to know who is the most influential member of the group. It may not be the person with the best title (an ad hoc group or project team may have been appointed to deal with this issue), and it almost certainly is not the one who speaks the most English. The company interpreter may be from the export department and very probably is not a person of either position or power. A top executive may drop in just to greet you. Don't exchange cards unless he offers his first.

In Japanese meetings you may find some different behavior that would be unusual in the West. People may close their eyes and look as though they're going to sleep. This is usually a sign of concentration. Higher-level executives, however, may actually fall asleep. Their job is not to focus on the issues at hand; it will be up to their subordinates to later brief them and others who could not attend. (Since their position requires a great deal of business entertaining, very late nights are the norm.)

During a meeting members of the Japanese team may break into side conversations or get up and use the telephone. People may come in and out. This is not uncommon behavior, so don't take it personally. Remember, too, there may be long periods of silence.

The Japanese team members may change from meeting to meeting. This can be a way of getting more people in their company to meet with you. In a system driven by consensus, it is essential that everyone be involved in and agree to company decisions.

In the interest of accurate communication, it can be a good idea to read the notes at the end of a meeting and have both parties initial them or to send a letter after you return home summarizing the main points as you see them. This is not common in Japan but is justified considering the language and cultural differences. Neither of these steps, however, will guarantee that the Japanese side will not later say they understood things differently, but these measures can catch some problems in the early stages.

Making the Presentation

During your meetings with the Japanese you may be required to give a presentation. Gearing it to your audience's expectations and needs will greatly contribute to its success.

Remember that presentations in Japan are a somewhat formal affair. Your clothing and your manner should convey this. If you can, have someone else introduce you. This adds to your credibility and lends an air of decorum to the atmosphere. Try to maintain a low-key and not overly animated style. Avoid talking while you are walking around, to pass out papers, for example. Don't tell jokes.

Organize your presentation in a simple, systematic way. Itemize points and ask your audience if they think they've been covered enough or if there are questions. It's perfectly acceptable to repeat or explain a point again for clarification, and this is preferable to asking, "Do you understand?" Speak slowly and downscale your language.

While you must cover each point carefully, these details must then be related back to the big picture. The Japanese take a holistic approach that requires understanding how the details will fit in with the overall objectives. They will want to understand the implications at many levels and how the details will affect concurrent projects as well as later ones. If you fail to continuously tie your points to the bigger perspective, the Japanese will ask questions later in the presentation that backtrack to earlier points you feel have been covered. Display patience in answering these questions. Until they have the big picture it will be difficult to make any true progress, and the sooner you can help them gain the understanding they need, the sooner you can move ahead. Showing that you are eager to listen to their issues will go a long way in helping to get them to reveal what still needs clarifying.

By all means, if possible use charts, films, handouts, slides, and graphs in your presentations. When communication is taking place in a foreign language, much is lost in the translation process. Trying to grasp meanings from verbal conversation becomes tiresome; visual support of your presentation is a welcome relief. It makes a lasting impression. Also, because verbosity is considered insincere, a picture, "worth a thousand words," is to be preferred.

One common type of graph used in Japan, especially when showing a comparison, is a radar graph. Intersecting lines are drawn to create a spoke-like diagram. Each spoke, representing an aspect of the item being compared, is then marked off in ascending increments usually up to 100. The appropriate number is plotted on each line, and these are then connected together and shaded in like a spider web. When the purpose is to contrast two or more products, companies, or whatever, the graphs are often superimposed—an easy way to see how they compare overall and where one might be weak. (See diagram.) Lotus had to modify their 1-2-3 software to accommodate the Japanese penchant for this type of graph.

Another common Japanese method of organizing data is the one-glance cover sheet (*ichi ran hyō*) for memoranda, proposals, and so on. This is a chart consisting of multiple squares that outline the various conclusions contained in the accompanying material. This allows the reader immediately to grasp the problem, the necessary action, and the result or prognosis of each item.

RADAR CHART

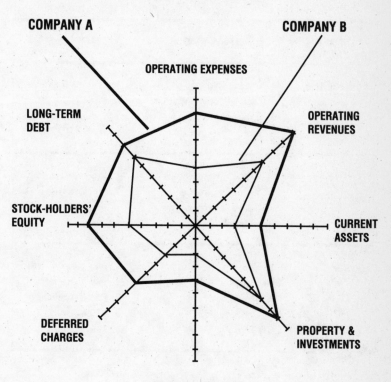

ANALYSIS FOR INCREASING CUSTOMER SATISFACTION

PROBLEM	ANALYSIS	ACTION
Quality	1. Lack of knowledge 2. Lack of communications 3. Careless mistakes 4. Lack of teamwork	1. Pre-meeting 2. Manual 3. Seminar
Delivery	1. Careless mistakes 2. Lack of teamwork 3. Delivery delay of raw material	1. Pre-meeting 2. Meeting with purchasing dept.
Price	1. Higher raw material cost 2. Overtime 3. Unneeded machine	1. Negotiation with purchasing dept. 2. Better planning 3. Teamwork inventory

The Japanese understand written English better than they do spoken English and will therefore get your point more clearly if you supply hard copies of your overheads for them to follow while you are speaking—and to refer to later.

Especially if you are giving a technical presentation, you may ultimately save yourself a tremendous amount of money if you make your overheads bilingual. Split your transparencies vertically, with English on one side and Japanese on the other. Your handout materials can be reproductions of your overheads.

Leave extra materials, including videos you have used, for others who did not attend the meeting. Also remember to follow through with anything you said you'll do. Seeing if you do can become a test of your reliability.

You may have noticed that while we tend to get directly to the point of a proposal then give the rationale, Japanese will usually give a long explanation first before getting to the actual proposal or the point. Again, most dialogue goes from the general to the specific rather than vice versa.

Another thing you may have noticed is that Japanese are great consumers of raw data, but dislike having others draw conclusions for them. To us this is a natural part of a sales presentation. The Japanese, however, find it inappropriate and patronizing.

Don't forget that the Japanese use the metric system. All measurements and weights should be converted. Temperatures should be represented in degrees Celsius.

18
Selling to the Japanese

While it may be more difficult working with a foreign client than a domestic one, especially in the beginning when you're learning the ropes, there can be extended dividends. If you make a sale to a foreign customer in your own country and do a good, professional job he or she is pleased with, that person is very likely to become your best advertisement. A recommendation from a compatriot goes a long way for newcomers to the area.

If you're working with a foreign customer on their turf, a job well done can unlock other doors and potentially open up a whole new market. In a recent survey conducted by the American Chamber of Commerce in Japan, 73 percent of the American companies in Japan said they thought they could attain higher profit rates there than back home. While it is a market that takes time to penetrate, statistics show that Japanese spend more per capita on American goods than Americans do on Japanese products (in 1989, $391 per Japanese buying American compared to $374 per American buying Japanese goods).

P.R. Means Personal Relations

The way business is transacted, as well as business priorities, are products of cultural attitudes. In America we focus on profits, usually generated through short-term commitments. The Japanese, however, traditionally focus on longevity through reinvestment of profits, market share, and reciprocal affiliations. This means developing long-term relationships not only with customers, but also with suppliers, distributors, bankers, and so on. (Out of economic necessity, however, a profit orientation is beginning to be more accepted.)

For this reason, in addition to selling your product or service you must also sell the relationship. The Japanese believe that if you build a good personal relationship, business will follow and that where there is goodwill and trust, details will be worked out naturally. Americans frequently forsake relationships to make a strictly bottom-line decision. It could be, however, that maintaining a relationship with someone you can count on to make compromises for you when you need them is worth more than short-term profits.

In many businesses the product life is too short to concentrate on it, which is another reason to focus on the relationship. If you represent a product that becomes obsolete or requires radical changes in a relatively short period of time, you will have to start all over again if you have made it your focus. However, if you have succeeded in portraying yourself as a reliable, astute partner, the new product becomes another aspect of that relationship, rather than you being an aspect of each product.

The Japanese are not averse to new products but are hesitant to work with new people. The most recent president of Nippon Telegraph and Telephone spent more than three months personally thanking 10,000 employees, customers, and suppliers—establishing a relationship—before he could begin his duties as president.

Honoring the Customer

In most business transactions, it's the buyer who has the upper hand. In Japan, this upper hand translates into a higher status as well. So if you are trying to sell something to a Japanese company, it behooves you to be more polite, more enthusiastic, and more willing to cater to your customer's every need than any competitor might be. And it's critical that you find out exactly what these needs are so you can appeal directly to them.

Keep in mind that business objectives for the Japanese often differ from those in the West. It could be a mistake to pin your sales pitch solely on profit. Prestige and market share can be significant issues. The Japanese also place a high priority on things such as steady employment for their people, controlled business growth, and competitive superiority. In order to best target their interest, try to find out ahead of time what their long- and short-term goals are, as well as any other "agenda" they may have. (See chapter 19 for sources of information.)

As part of your long-term strategy, make your company's name synonymous with quality and prestige. In a competitive market, quality of the product must be a given—it's service and customization that give you the edge. The National Bicycle Industrial Company, a manufacturer in Kubuko, Japan, is the epitome of customization and service. Within two weeks of ordering, a custom-made bicycle can be produced precisely to fit one's measurements. Prices are only 10 percent more than ready-made bicycles, and the consumer is able to choose from more than 11 million variations in models.

If you are trying to sell a product to a Japanese customer who already has a supplier, in addition to being able to convince the buyer that your product has significant advantages, you will need to be able to supply any other products or "freebies," goodwill gifts provided by their current supplier. Also important is that you may have to figure out how they can make the switch without causing a loss of face for the current supplier, such as offering something their supplier can't provide as part of your package. It is important to genuinely care about the position the Japanese are in and the consequences they may face in making a decision to switch to your company or accept a new product line. It rarely is as simple as just buying and selling. Japanese are conscious of being judged by their peers on what position they are putting others in if they make a change. They must consider all their bases before deciding, or else risk their standing with those who have a vested interest in maintaining the present arrangement.

Soft Selling

A hard sell is not only offensive in Japan but can be taken to mean that without such a hard push, no one would buy your product.

A low-key sales pitch—using objective information, not pressure, to convince—meets with most success. Japanese are not accustomed to aggressive American techniques that use a persuasive, "winning" argument.

It's thought that a product should be able to stand on its own merits. If you use biased information to describe your product, your credibility will be damaged and what you say will lose influence. Rather than declaring yours is "the best on the market," it would be much better to say, "We sold two million units last year. As you know, our closest competitor sold less than a million." At the same time, be careful not to put down competing products. In fact, the Japanese will respect you for your honesty if you mention the assets of the competition.

Provide Reference Materials

Let your documentation do most of the talking. Remember, verbosity is considered insincere and humility is admired. It's better to avoid appearing to be self-centered by talking too much about your position or product. Others' opinions of your product, however, can be very valuable—they give credence to your claims. Published articles from trade or technical periodicals with references to your company or products thus enhance your credibility.

Have important materials translated into Japanese. This shows your commitment to working with them. If you are relying on your client company to do this for those who do not speak English, you lose control of the quality and timing of the translation. The translator in their organization may not be clear on all the terminology and may already be overworked, and the resulting translation could set your project back quite a bit. Expensive English-language brochures can have a Japanese insert.

Exhibit Flexibility

While some foreign products may be successfully sold in Japan just as they are, others may need modification. There are countless failure stories attributable to either poor market research or inflexibility on the part of the U.S. manufacturers. It's unreasonable, for example, to think you can sell many cars when the steering wheel is on the wrong side. In many cases, however, the required alteration may not be so obvious. A major American cosmetics company failed miserably in Japan because they had not taken into account the Japanese skin tone. Taste in food and drink may vary greatly from your domestic market and, in fact, even varies within Japan. Some Japanese products—instant noodles for example—are flavored slightly differently for the Tokyo and Osaka areas.

It may be necessary to tailor not only your product but also other conditions to suit Japanese custom and taste. The Japanese are used to frequent deliveries, taking merchandise on consignment, having extensive incentive plans, and receiving much longer credit terms than are Americans. Not uncommon is the "pregnant" note, for example, which matures in nine months.

The usage of an English word in Japan may differ greatly from its original meaning. Some may be quite amusing to you. One bar advertises "Special cocktail for ladies with nuts." And there's a bridal shop in the Ginza with a window sign that reads, "For your wedding best. It's a fluke!"—well, maybe it is. Just remember that we do this with foreign words as well. Make sure that any English words you plan to identify with your product carry the same meaning to the Japanese. For example, in Japan the English word "smart" refers to appearance rather than intelligence.

Packaging and Appearance

In Japan, a product's container is often as important as its contents. As elsewhere, packaging conveys the prestige associated with the product. But, as with the Japanese cuisine, in which even ordinary meals should appeal to the eye as much as the palate, the appearance makes the product.

The quality of your product and company is reflected in the materials you present. Packaging and appearance can play a significantly influential role with your Japanese counterparts and with consumers. Make sure your brochure projects the best possible image. Don't skimp in this area.

Trade fairs are another example. In comparison to equivalent American firms, Japanese companies spend much more money on booths, using an abundance of lights and high-tech gadgetry to draw people in. Their booths are not only larger but are staffed by higher-level people, usually at the managerial level and often above.

After-Sales Service

You must show that you'll be able to provide product and relationship maintenance with after-sales service. In fact, "after-service" is considered an essential part of product sales. You need to convince them that you'll still be there to service the product later on.

As an example of the type of after-service the Japanese are used to, Pacific Beach Printers, a small print shop in San Diego, had a Hashimoto printing press that broke down while still under warranty. When the Japanese manufacturer was contacted they dispatched two service men the same day. Unfortunately the service men ended up in New York by mistake but caught the next plane to San Diego. They arrived at 8:30 P.M. and insisted on going straight to work without stopping at the hotel or eating. In twenty minutes the machine was working. They continued to do repairs and extensive upgrading modifications with only hand tools until the owner insisted they get some sleep at 3:00 in the morning.

A recent survey highlights the importance of after-sales service. When asked what criteria they used to select a supplier, American firms indicated that price and quality were of primary concern. The Japanese response, however, reflects their preference for a dependable relationship: quick and conscientious responses to specific requests, good follow-up service, and reliability.

Japanese expect you to be punctual about any agreements you have made, no matter how informally, regarding things like deliveries and permits. If *anything* is going to be delayed, try to let them know as soon as possible. They often function on a slim time margin to cut down on warehousing, and what's more, something you haven't foreseen may be tied to timing. For example, if you've told them you expect to receive a building permit by a certain time, they may be planning a ground-breaking ceremony to coincide with that date.

Customer Relations

In many countries the customer is considered "king," but in Japan, "the customer is God!" *(Okyaku-sama wa kami-sama desu.)* Japanese are masters of the art of making others feel special and important. This personal attention makes all the difference. Japanese customers like to believe they are the most important person to you, or that the deal with them is the most important thing you and your company are engaged in at the moment.

After the sell has been made, the Japanese buyer will expect the seller's sense of obligation to grow stronger. Even after the monetary transaction, the seller still feels indebted to the buyer. Japanese buyers may seem demanding by our standards because they are used to the sellers bending over backward to show their gratitude and continued commitment. For example, some Japanese realtors in the United States will go into the home after escrow has closed and have the utilities turned on for the buyer as an after-sales service. They understand the "real" relationship begins after the sale is completed.

Be diplomatic, be cooperative, and be committed. Remember that the customer is always right and results often don't come quickly. You may need to be responsive to requests that take time, that won't increase your immediate sales, or that seem irrelevant. But by doing so you create "face" and show a spirit of unconditional cooperation and of being a team player.

On the other hand, don't expect applause from your Japanese counterparts on your successes. They rarely congratulate an individual's achievement, such as exceeding a sales goal.

Setting Up an Office in Japan

Your presence in Japan is essential if you are trying to establish contacts and build stronger relationships with your Japanese clients.

However, if you find setting up an office in Tokyo is more than your budget can handle, you may want to consider one of the business centers designed for those unable to make a large capital investment. These do not convey the appropriate image for a large corporation but are a good first step for smaller companies and entrepreneurs. Many of these cater to foreign businesses that will later move on to larger offices or that are in Japan for only a short period of time.

Services vary from center to center. Many provide a direct telephone line and a receptionist who answers the telephone with the company's name. Others provide access to fax machines, conference rooms, or translation services for a small fee. See appendix C for a few of the better-known centers in the Tokyo area.

If your company wants a stronger presence in Japan than just a temporary office, you should consider opening a representative office there. These offices function as liaisons, engaging in activities such as market research, information gathering, and making business contacts. One step further would be opening a branch office in Japan, which could play a larger role than the representative office but which is also subject to further regulation.

If your commitment to Japan is very serious, your company may wish to incorporate as a *kabushiki kaisha* (K.K.), which is like an American corporation with a board of directors and shareholders who have limited liability for the company.

19
Working the Angles

According to Herb Cohen in *You Can Negotiate Anything* (1980), power, time, and information are the three crucial elements of every negotiation. Because the Japanese consider themselves poor negotiators in a confrontational way (known also as the Western way), they have learned to manipulate these basic aspects of negotiating to their advantage.

Power

As discussed earlier, the Japanese prefer to work in teams rather than individually. The strength of numbers is a powerful tool that the Japanese understand very well. It's something that Westerners doing business in Japan will have to counter in kind. (See chapter 15 for tips on putting your team together.)

If you must go to Japan to negotiate, the disadvantage of location is obvious. If the option is open to you, invite them to visit outside Japan, on your home base or at least halfway—in Hawaii, for example, or Hong Kong or Guam. If you do go to Japan, meeting in a room you've arranged at your hotel, your branch office, or even a restaurant will help to neutralize their advantage.

Having a competitive product with a good reputation and in high demand, of course, gives you an advantage. On the other hand, appearing to be at a disadvantage can be used to your advantage. It brings down the other side's guard and encourages them to help you by providing information and even advice. In such a situation, your asking innocuous questions can elicit valuable data and may expose some empty claims.

On the personal level, as your negotiations evolve you could try applying a subtle use of power such as more direct eye contact to put pressure on members of the other side. Remember that impatience and anxiety send the message that the other party is in control. When negotiating, displaying impatience may prompt your Japanese counterpart to hold out for more concessions.

Time

Whenever the other side knows that your deadline is earlier than theirs, you're at a disadvantage. Since you know that things take longer in Japan, your first strategy should be to extend your deadline. Then try not to divulge what your deadline is. Because the length of your hotel reservation will be open knowledge, make your reservation either for much less time than you intend to stay, whereupon you can be nonchalant about postponing your departure as many times as you have to, or make your reservation for much longer than you actually intend to stay. As your deadline approaches, don't let it show. Be patient. Stay cool and act as if you've got at least as much time as they.

Your hosts may overwhelm you if you take a business trip to Japan. They will see to it that almost every minute of your day and night is filled with activity—whether it be having meetings, traveling to a destination, or indulging in lavish entertainment. While it may be difficult, try not to let the pace overwhelm you. Be forewarned that you will probably be in constant motion. It is essential for you to take time to meet with your team and to get enough rest. (The Japanese may have a tag team fulfilling the various roles.)

Information

The Japanese will have obtained detailed information about your products, people, business, and reputation. You will be in a compromised position if you are not as well informed. The more you know about the other side's goals, priorities, finances, time constraints, and commitments, the better position you'll be in. Do as much research as you possibly can ahead of time. Learn to talk little and ask open-ended questions to gather more information during meetings.

Very often our marketing, manufacturing, and R&D departments are not in close contact with each other. This means that after negotiating with your marketing department, the Japanese may talk directly with your manufacturing department and be alarmed if they have a different opinion or story. A similar problem can arise if you have more than one group going to Japan; if they haven't been in close contact, subsequent groups may be redundant or deliver a different message. The Japanese look for consistency of information as an indication of reliability.

A central source for monitoring information could help. One good method is to keep a file containing all the latest issues and decisions. It could have up-dated, pertinent information about the company, such as if it has just been listed on the stock exchange, relevant information about their team members, and gifts that have been exchanged, noting what was well received. The names of everyone in your company who has connection with the Japanese company, including the dates and subjects of interaction, should be included so interested parties can get more detailed information. This file could also reiterate sensitive information that is not to be discussed (or perhaps some relevant information that was inadvertently gathered from a trip to Japan). These steps will help to give you a unified attitude and consistent strategy.

If you are concerned about piracy, have your product patented or trademarked in Japan. If your prospective customer asks for blueprints that you don't feel comfortable sharing, tell him they are classified. As anywhere in the world, one must be wary of con men.

Throughout the negotiating process, remember that friendliness and effusive politeness are just that. Don't read into them friendship or a deeper respect that might not be there. Play by *their* rules. Be formal, polite, humble—but be shrewd.

GOOD SOURCES OF INFORMATION INCLUDE:

Japan External Trade Organization (JETRO)/
   Ministry of International Trade and Industry (MITI)
The Japanese Embassy/Japanese Consulates
The Japanese Chamber of Commerce
The Department of Commerce/International Trade
   Administration
The American Chamber of Commerce in Japan (ACCJ)
The American Embassy's Business Resource Section
State Representative's Office in Japan
Small Business Administration
Industrial or Trade Associations
Annual Reports and Standard Trade Index
Competing Companies
Freight Forwarders, Banks, Accounting, and Trading Companies
Their Customers and Suppliers
Consultants and Corporate Credit Agencies
Local Trade Centers, Trade Agencies, and Trade Magazines
U.S. Japan–America Societies
Japanese University Professors
Your Go-between
Japanese Periodicals and Newspapers printed in English

   See appendices for addresses, useful reference books,
                and other information.

20
Closing the Deal

There will come a time toward the end of negotiations when both sides will have to whittle down their demands and desires. Concessions will have to be made to reach a workable agreement.

Your Japanese counterparts will want to save face for both sides by not letting it appear that either was forced into a compromise, so avoid using a tit-for-tat approach. Subtle bending on both sides will yield the most desirable results.

If at this time you feel you are not getting what you need, it may be time to use your go-between or to talk informally with one member of their team. If these are not possibilities, you have no recourse other than to make gentle suggestions. At the end of a meeting, for example, you could allude to what you desire, prefacing it with, "You might want to consider . . ." In any case, let it appear that they came up with the idea themselves.

The Westerner's greatest mistake is likely to be impatience, especially at times when the Japanese are silent. Do not assume they are rejecting the points under discussion, and don't give away too much just to get the conversation going again. Maybe you will be able to tolerate these silent periods better by imagining they're trying to figure out a way to give in to you without losing face themselves. Perhaps they are. (A friend of mine who is married to a Japanese claims this advice saved her marriage.)

Throughout the negotiations, it is not uncommon for them to ask you for what seems an excessive amount of data. There may be a number of reasons for this. In some cases, they may really require more information to make a decision. From their point of view, they need a lot of backup to justify the transaction within their company and to save face for all involved, should the venture fail. Alternatively, asking for more information may be a way to force you into lowering your price, in much the same way silence is used as a negotiating tactic. In another case, it may be a way to put off saying no.

Much of this data may also be needed for the Ministry of International Trade and Industry (MITI), which often demands copious amounts of detailed information before approving the importation of a new product.

Concessions

The offering of concessions differs in Japan and America in a couple of ways. In *Smart Bargaining*, John Graham and Yoshi Sano discuss the sequential versus the holistic negotiation style. The American style of negotiating is to determine points one by one. If there are ten items to be negotiated, you are halfway to your goal when you've covered five. This is the sequential style or linear approach. The Japanese have a holistic style, discussing points in relationship to the package as a whole and then making all concessions at the end. This means that if you have been making concessions as you went along, you will be in trouble at the conclusion when they will expect you to concede more to get concessions from them. The hard part about this for Americans is that it is difficult for them to judge progress. The advantage, however, is once the big picture is gained, trade-offs can be made in unrelated areas where each side gives up less of what is important to them.

Another difference is that in America, posturing and intimidation often play a role in negotiations, and sometimes the desired results are gained by making the "opponent" feel uncomfortable. The reverse is true in Japan. The Japanese build a partnership with and gain the trust of their negotiating counterparts. Again, we frequently take an adversarial position, forgetting that when a long-term relationship is the object it is not advisable to fight for short-term gains at the expense of the other party.

One sign of progress may be participation by higher-level managers. Another may be a zeroing in on specific issues. If you are unclear as to where things stand or what is holding the negotiations up, use informal channels (going out for a drink) or try to get your introducer or a mutual friend to find out what's going on. It may be necessary to bring in a go-between (*chūkai-sha*) or to bring your two CEOs together for a ceremonial meeting.

In offering concessions, the Japanese may tell you they are making generous concessions of goodwill. This is often part of the ritual, and "final offers" are not always final offers. Be sure to ask questions before you counteroffer so you can gain insight into what their expectations really are and find creative and workable solutions. Just be sure that in your "solutions" you do not back the other side into a corner.

If it becomes apparent that things will not work out, it is important to avoid burning bridges behind you. Be sure to thank them for the opportunity to discuss the proposal and assure them that you look forward to a chance to work with them in the future.

Signing the Contract

When a satisfactory arrangement for both sides has been reached, it's contract time. At this stage, rather than having a let's-get-it-over-with attitude, the Japanese will be more likely to view the situation as the true beginning of the relationship.

Traditionally in Japan a "gentleman's agreement" has been quite sufficient. The Japanese do realize, however, that when dealing with a foreign company they will eventually have to sign a contract. Just remember that they will not take this document as seriously as they take the verbal agreement. The contract should cover the main points but should also leave room for flexibility that allows both sides to cope with changing situations.

Contracts replete with legalese may be unacceptable to a Japanese partner. The American tendency toward contracts that clearly outline legal repercussions should one party not be able to meet its obligations has been compared to planning the end of a relationship before it even begins. The Japanese will want to feel that they have embarked upon an ongoing harmonious relationship. Japanese contracts, even with foreign companies, tend to be short by Western standards. For example, a major contract with the Japanese may be only three pages, while a similar circumstance would require 100 pages in America.

Probably the most important aspect of their version of a contract is an agreement to renegotiate, should circumstances change. Westerners tend to expend a great deal of energy trying to hold others to contracts even when unforeseeable events make it impossible or unfair to do so. In the Japanese way of thinking it's the relationship you're committing to. You will be better off at this time if you indicate a willingness to renegotiate points in question.

To the Japanese, a formal ceremony is an important final step in the sealing of a pact. If the deal being closed is of significant financial magnitude, the ceremony should be attended by high-ranking personnel as well as those who participated in the actual negotiations. In Japan there will be many speeches, gifts, and photographs, followed by a magnificent reception. If the signing takes place in your own country, you may be able to get away with an abbreviated version, but some sort of formal ceremony and reception will be necessary.

This should be followed up with a warm letter from those involved. A formal letter of felicitation and optimism should also be sent from your chief executive officer to theirs. This, however, cannot take the place of frequent face-to-face contact.

Backing Out

If at any time you feel you must back out or refuse a deal, it is imperative that in doing so you save face for your counterparts. If you think the real reason for your withdrawal would cause them embarrassment, make some sort of innocuous excuse. Tell them you need more time to consider things, or simply say vaguely, "It seems difficult."

Refusals must be indirect and are best left to a go-between to communicate for you. Just make sure that your go-between is very clear on the reasons why you are backing out.

A breach of contract will soon become common knowledge in

Japan. All kinds of information gets around in Japan, and gets around quickly. One of the major American oil companies made a financial decision that would affect two Japanese banks it worked with in California. Although it was after business hours, they called one and discussed the situation. As it was very late by the time the conversation ended, they decided to contact the other bank in the morning. Within minutes after leaving the office, however, the CFO received a call on his car phone from the other Japanese bank, wanting to know what was going on.

Following Up

Once an agreement is concluded, a "maintenance" phase must be initiated to make sure the relationship stays warm and friendly. Do not ignore this last stage.

Send letters of gratitude to everyone who was involved. An album of photographs you have taken of formal and informal meetings leading up to the successful agreement is, again, a nice touch.

Later on, personal notes from time to time will be required for maintaining a sense of camaraderie. If you lapse into treating your agreement with them as strictly a business relationship, you in turn will be viewed as just another foreign company, including all the negative connotations that perception brings.

IV

THE SOCIAL SIDE OF BUSINESS

21
The Art of Entertaining

Social drinking and entertaining play a significant role in Japanese business culture. In fact, going out drinking together with your friends, colleagues, and clients is virtually an indispensable part of doing business. Trust and rapport are established most quickly during nonbusiness hours. Without these only the minimum can be accomplished, so it's highly advisable that you accept every invitation you receive and participate to the best of your ability.

As a nation, Japan spends more money on entertainment (according to the National Tax Administration Agency, $72 million a day) than it does on defense or education. Western businessmen are not unfamiliar with this social ritual, especially in the form of cocktail parties, but in Japan not only the protocol but also the institution of drinking is prescribed.

Drinking as Cultural Intermission

For the Japanese male, social drinking is an outlet. At the heart of this ritual is the old inflexible, unwritten law that surface harmony must be maintained at all costs. Naturally, this is very stressful, as one must constantly suppress his emotions and opinions for the sake of group harmony.

Intoxication is the time, or state, in which a Japanese man can express himself rather freely and with impunity—an opportunity to show his true nature without fear of repercussion. It is a time of "intermission" when many of the rules of etiquette go out the window and the normal restrictive rules of behavior don't apply.

Getting drunk, or at least giving the appearance of it, is not only condoned, it is actually encouraged as a means of bonding. The Japanese will proceed to sing, laugh, even dance and play in such a totally uninhibited manner that it may seem childlike to the circumspect Western businessman.

By all means, participate as much as possible. Besides the enjoyment of indulging in a type of fun you probably haven't experienced in many years, you will, more importantly, earn the trust of your companions. This is because they feel that some aspects of one's true personality and feelings will surface during a friendly session of drinking camaraderie, establishing deeper understanding and a good basis for friendly business negotiations. What's more, because it's thought a person's "soul" comes out when he drinks, if someone is not willing to participate, he is often suspected of having something to hide.

In addition to uninhibited fun, you may be surprised to witness other atypical behavior. For example, it would not be unusual to see your associates stray from their normally impeccable manners and indulge in unruly behavior, uncharacteristic frankness and complaints about or even to their superiors. Under the pretense of being drunk, a person can register grievances that he couldn't normally, but still he must be careful.

At all times remember that this is only the intermission and that the unwritten rule is that nothing silly that might be said during this time is to be taken seriously. If the singing and camaraderie seem childish or ridiculous, it is essential that you keep an open mind and learn to roll with the events of the evening. Appreciate the moment in its cultural context, and don't think about how your peers back home would judge it. If it gets agonizing, keep your goals in mind and see this as a means to that end. Remember, tomorrow these will be serious businessmen. The day after your night of drinking you should not refer to things that happened or were said, except to thank your host for the occasion.

Participation is the key to a successful night of drinking with the Japanese, but be sure to gauge your behavior. While your Japanese counterparts may be joking and appear to be informal, behavior such as causing another person to be humiliated is still unacceptable.

Generally bar hopping (*hashigo*) is only for the boys—or those involved in the business dealings. If your spouse has been invited along for dinner it would be best for her (or him) to excuse herself when the meal is over. The men then usually go on for hours, stopping for a couple of drinks and snacks at one place after another, frequenting their favorite places until the wee hours of the morning.

If you are in any sort of critical phase with the Japanese (such as negotiating or building the relationship) it would be best to forego bringing your spouse to Japan at all. If she (or he) has accompanied you, make separate plans for her in the evenings and decline polite invitations from your Japanese colleagues with, "I'm so sorry, she has tickets for the theater."

While it's not traditional, younger Japanese men and those who have spent much time abroad may plan an evening that will include your wife as well as their own. While some Japanese women welcome this type of social activity, others are still uncomfortable with it.

It's not unusual for normally reserved Japanese to ask personal questions of each other or of foreigners, such as, "Why aren't you married?" or "How much do you make?" A common response is avoiding the question altogether or answering in a vague manner. I have found that the best response to the latter question is, "Not enough. How much do you make?"

As a Western businesswoman, if you would like to join the men after hours, by all means do so. You don't want to miss the opportunity to enhance your business relationship and establish an informal flow of information. It would be good to show some restraint, though, like not drinking anything stronger than your host. Remember, the situation is not a drinking contest. Loosen up a little, but don't lose control. Returning to your hotel earlier than the men is perfectly acceptable. Besides being viewed as appropriately modest behavior, the next day *you'll* have a clear head.

Be aware that your Japanese counterparts may appear to be more inebriated than they really are. Appearing more drunk than you actually are allows you to participate to the fullest while sparing your body the "*sake* slam" and jeopardizing your negotiating stamina for the following day.

Drinking Etiquette

The indigenous alcoholic beverage of Japan is *sake* (pronounced sah-kay, not sah-kee), a rice wine, which is stronger than American beer or wine (between 15 and 20 percent alcohol). It is heated gently in a ceramic vase-like container to 110–120 degrees Fahrenheit and then drunk from miniature cups called *sakazuki* or *o-choko*.

As with other things Japanese, there is a strict etiquette to drinking. There are basically three rules to your social imbibing. The first is: Don't pour your own drink. The second is: Refill drinks for your colleagues or friends around you. Bottles of alcohol are ordered for the table rather than for the individual, so you can simply pick up any bottle and pour for the other person. Third: While another person is pouring for you, you should lift your glass. Women often use both hands when pouring a drink and holding a glass, while men just use one unless pouring for someone of much higher status. Of course, as people get more inebriated the etiquette often deteriorates.

One of your companions may honor you by presenting you with his empty cup, then filling it for you to drink from. When you have finished, return it and fill it for him. You may wish to present your own cup to your host or some other special person. If there is a bowl of water present, the shared cup is rinsed after each use.

A caution: Pace yourself during these nights of drinking. Since you and your companions will be continuously filling each other's glasses, it is often hard to determine just how much you've had to drink. Remember that warm drinks such as *sake* go down smoothly and may have a delayed effect on your body. Beer is often drunk at the same time as *sake*, and this only contributes to the chance of unpleasant consequences.

If you cannot tolerate alcohol, just touch the glass to your lips or sip it lightly after the kanpai (the toast), keeping your glass full most of the way. Keeping your glass as full as possible keeps it from being refilled. If you must refuse a drink, prepare a good excuse. A common excuse for not drinking is: "A liver ailment—no alcohol, doctor's orders" (in Japanese, *Dokutā sutoppu*). Most places can provide oolong tea (*ūron cha*) or ginger ale or other soft drinks instead. If a bar says they have no soft drinks, they can still provide the mineral water used in scotch and water.

Even if you do not drink, try to get into the spirit of the evening by pouring drinks for others and loosening up.

The Japanese generally do not invite others to their homes for cocktail parties because their homes are very small. Consequently, social drinking is done in bars, clubs, and cabarets. These are all part of the *mizu shobai* (water trade), so called because this environment relaxes and cleanses the spirit like water, leaving no trace of tension.

In the clubs, more whiskey than beer or *sake* is consumed. Most Japanese drink their whiskey "cut" with water—*mizu wari*. If you prefer your whiskey on the rocks, ask for it *on-za-rokku*.

Drinking excursions are not the time to continue your business conversations or to talk about any other serious matter. It is a time to relax, have fun, and cultivate friendship and trust, which, as should be clear by now, are the foundations for successfully doing business in Japan. When you have developed a strong personal relationship with an individual you may talk *honne* while drinking one on one. In groups, however, the social time is for developing relationships.

Singing Bars

One form of entertainment that has won considerable popularity in recent years is *karaoke* (*kara* meaning "empty," *oke* meaning "orchestra"). What this amounts to is a way for people to live out, for a few heartfelt minutes, their fantasies of stardom by crooning their rendition of a favorite song to taped background instrumentation. It's the chance to entertain your friends, colleagues, and other patrons of the nightclub as well as yourself, and that makes it fun for all. The words are usually written on a video monitor in front of you and often projected along with various scenes on a larger screen for other guests to view. In smaller establishments that don't have video *karaoke* sets, the lyrics can be found in songbooks.

It cannot be overemphasized how participation in activities such as this can later turn out to be a great asset. You build camaraderie by being vulnerable together. In fact, you almost get more "points" for being willing to join in on the fun in spite of a serious lack of talent. Remember, it's all in the name of establishing bonds and showing what a good sport you are.

You will almost always be able to find a few enduring Western popular songs like "I Left My Heart in San Francisco," "My Way," "Yesterday," and "Bridge Over Troubled Water." The words on their videos or in their books, however, will most likely be in Japanese, so be prepared with a few verses that you can at least fake.

Some *karaoke* videos are quite risqué by our standards, which could create some discomfort for you in mixed company. Japanese women, however, while perhaps displaying a proper degree of embarrassment, will not find them offensive or "dirty."

Karaoke, incidentally, has most recently made its appearance in homes and in cars, where a portable microphone creates the desired effect. Company trips in which a large bus is used for transportation may also feature *karaoke* with popular traveling songs. *Karaoke* is so popular that practice booths can be rented by the hour.

Being a Guest

When a guest of the Japanese, it is important to be just that and allow them to take care of matters without consulting or informing you. Westerners often feel compelled to try to find out what the plans are, and these constant questions can be quite annoying to Japanese. There may not be any plans laid out at all. The next event may be discussed or decided only when that time arises, as spontaneity is often part of the spirit. Your role as guest is to enjoy each new affair, like the subsequent act in a play, without asking what is going to happen next. Letting go of control, or even knowledge of what is going on, can be hard for many Westerners, but it is important to go with the flow. As with many interactions with Japanese friends and counterparts, looking for emotional attunement rather than intellectual explanations may bring you the most satisfaction.

The time that you can ask questions is when you are not clear on the protocol (such as how to eat a certain food). Japanese appreciate your desire to understand the conventions and don't expect you to "wing it."

Remember that the little things you do go a long way toward communicating your gratitude and sincerity. When your host sees you off, don't forget to turn back one last time to say good-bye. When being seen off at an elevator, your Japanese host will usually bow just before the doors close and you should acknowledge this with a return bow. Remembering to say thank you again the next time you see your host or hostess is essential.

22
Dining

Most cultures place value on "breaking bread together" to enhance friendships, and business people everywhere punctuate their schedules with lunch and dinner engagements. Japan is no exception. In fact, due to its strong emphasis on creating friendly relationships with all business partners, you may find yourself being wined and dined more than once before you even begin preliminary discussions.

Proper table manners are essential. Westerners don't warm to foreigners who won't use knives and forks any more than Japanese do to foreigners who won't use chopsticks. And that's the least of it.

Rituals of the Meal

The Japanese take a lot of pride in their traditional meal. Great pains are taken to make every morsel a masterpiece of subtle elegance in both appearance and taste. In like fashion, the etiquette for "receiving the feast" is somewhat involved.

The first thing you will receive is an *o-shibori*, a small damp towel, usually warm or hot, on an oblong tray. This is to cleanse your hands, although men in particular will be seen on less formal occasions refreshing their faces as well. When you are finished, fold the towel and put it back on its container. (Traditional Japanese restaurants do not have napkins and do not always have *o-shibori* either.)

A typical meal (such as the traditional, formal *kaiseki ryōri* meal) arrives in a variety of small dishes on a lacquered tray. If they are on a lacquered tray, the dishes are not to be removed from the tray. In the front part of the tray may be two covered bowls: rice on the left and soup on the right. Nothing should be taken from either of these bowls without picking up the bowl and holding it while you eat from it.

To be perfectly correct, pick up your chopsticks with the right hand palm down. Take the tips with the left hand palm up and then adjust the sticks properly in the right hand. If they come in a paper cover, they are the disposable type that must be separated before using.

Remove the cover of your soup bowl. If the cover of your soup won't come off easily, squeeze the sides of the bowl gently to break the vacuum seal. Pick up the bowl and place it on your left palm. The right hand is used to steady the bowl. Take a sip from the bowl, pick out a morsel with your chopsticks, and put the bowl back down. Spoons are not used with the soup.

Have some rice next. As you did with your soup bowl, you must lift your rice bowl in order to eat from it. Holding the bowl in your left hand, take a small mouthful of rice with your chopsticks and bring it to your mouth. Continuing to hold the rice bowl in your left hand, you may now proceed to eat a little of each dish at a time, taking no more than three bites of a dish at one time, rather than finishing one off and moving to the next one. Eat bit by bit from all the dishes on the tray, except the pickles, which traditionally are to be eaten last. Take a mouthful of rice between bites of the other dishes to cleanse your palate. It is considered improper not to do so. Often the rice bowl is held while taking items from dishes on the tray and put down only to pick up the soup, which also should last throughout the meal.

It's likely that *sashimi*, sliced raw fish, will come with this meal. Fish prepared by the Japanese is very fresh and has no fishy odor or taste, but if you find the thought of raw fish unappetizing, the best thing you can do is work on changing your attitude. Put your cultural prejudice aside (many Japanese have a hard time with the thought of eating raw cauliflower) and you may even be pleasantly surprised.

On the plate of fish you will usually find a pile of grated green horseradish and a variety of seaweed. Some or all of the horseradish (*wasabi*) is to be added to the accompanying small dish of soy sauce, but start with a small amount, as it's hotter than you might expect. Thoroughly dip the *sashimi* in your soy sauce before eating it, and have some rice in between different types of fish.

A great deal of importance is placed on rice, the staff of life. When you have finished your other dishes you may eat the salted pickles with the last of your rice. The traditional and subtle way to indicate you'd like a second helping of rice is to leave a little bit of rice in your bowl. These days, however, it is also acceptable to simply ask for more.

When you have finished, replace the covers on your soup and rice bowls. The proper way to say "thank you" at the end of a meal is to say with a bow, "*Go chisō sama deshita*," meaning "It was a treat."

A Caution on Chopsticks

Since you will be eating your meals with chopsticks, it is best if you've spent some time practicing with them. Don't worry if you make a few mistakes—no one will expect you to do everything perfectly. The important thing is to stay relaxed. Don't make your hosts uncomfortable by being uncomfortable yourself.

The Japanese themselves adhere to a much more elaborate code of etiquette than is necessary for a foreigner. Just to avoid making some really gross errors, however, here are a few dos and don'ts:

- Don't leave your chopsticks sticking up in your rice bowl— this is the way of offering rice to the dead.
- Because rice is used to cleanse the palate, sauces, such as soy sauce, are never poured over rice.
- Never take something off a serving dish with your own chopsticks unless you turn them around and use the large, dull ends. This is done for the sake of hygiene.
- Always use serving chopsticks if they are present.
- Never dally over dishes trying to figure out what's in them. Decide, for the sake of international relations, world peace, and smart business, that you are going to eat whatever it is and then proceed. Don't insult your hosts by saying or im-

plying that you didn't like something they served or ordered for you. (Remember what you think of people who refuse to try different foods in your own home.) Showing genuine interest in the food by wanting to know more about it is, of course, not considered rude.

• Do not blow your nose at the table.

Sushi—Not Just Raw Fish

One Japanese delicacy that has become fashionable in the West is *sushi*. *Nigirizushi* is raw or cooked fish, shrimp, eel, squid, or octopus on little blocks of delicately flavored rice. In *makizushi*, rice and a vegetable or fish are rolled up in a sheet of seaweed, then sliced into pieces.

At a *sushi* bar, the pieces of *sushi* come in pairs. They're served with finely sliced pinkish ginger and a small dish for soy sauce. The ginger is used to cleanse the palate between different types of *sushi*. The green horseradish will already have been applied between the fish and the rice. If you want more horseradish, you'll have to ask for it in Japan (unlike in Japanese restaurants in the States, where, because of its popularity, extra horseradish is the usual accompaniment). Try your *sushi* before asking for extra horseradish; it may be quite hot enough. A hint: Breathe through your mouth to keep the dragon out of your nose. If you get too much horseradish, hit yourself at the base of your skull to calm its effects.

Since you always receive a small damp towel at a *sushi* bar, it is perfectly all right to eat *sushi* with your hands at a *sushi* bar. The easiest way is to take it by the far end and turn it over to dip it in your sauce. With *sushi*, it's the fish, not the rice, that's dipped in the soy sauce. Put the *sushi* in your mouth with the rice side up and the fish side down, so that the fish is first to touch your tongue. It is preferable to eat the whole piece of *sushi* at one time rather than in bites. Avoid putting more soy sauce in your small dish than you need. Dipping your sushi into a deep reservoir is messy and wasting soy sauce is frowned upon.

Sushi chefs are at some liberty to adjust the bill of their patrons. A survey indicated they give the most discount to those who request their *sushi* in the proper order. The best sequence begins with mild-flavored *sushi*, such as egg or sole, progresses to the stronger flavors, such as eel and yellowtail, and ends with cucumber (*kappa-maki*) or pickle (*o-shinko maki*). If, however, you come across as "showing off" or being arrogant, the chef's billing prerogative could work against you. Baked egg and mackerel *sushi* will tell you the quality of the chef.

Many *sushi* chefs are glad to join you in a glass of beer or cup of *sake* if you offer them some. One thing they don't like is for you to give them back the dirty dishes. Someone else will usually collect these. They also don't like to handle money when the check is paid. Money is considered dirty and separate from their "craft."

If you absolutely can't bear raw fish, try *ebi* (cooked shrimp), *tamago* (egg prepared like an omelet), *maguro* (tuna—raw, but it has a mild flavor), *anago* and *unagi* (eel, broiled with a sweet sauce), or *kyuri* (cucumber).

Noodles

The etiquette of eating Japanese noodles also deserves special mention. There are many varieties of noodles (*soba, udon, somen*) in Japan—served hot in a soup, fried, or cold with a broth to dip them in.

Eating noodles with chopsticks is simply a matter of practice. The only trick is to keep your chopsticks open around the noodles as you suck them in and to keep them from wrapping around your cheeks if you inhale too fast. Slurp, even if you've spent years trying not to—in Japan a slurp is a sign of pleasure and appreciation. Besides, sucking in air with the soup as you slurp your noodles allows you to eat them while they're still very hot.

Other Foods

There are many different kinds of foods in Japan, but each restaurant usually has only one type, such as bowl dishes or *sushi*. In other words, you won't be able to get *soba* at a *sushi* bar or *yakitori* (grilled chicken) at a *soba* shop. The plastic models in the display cases outside most restaurants will give you an idea of what kind of food is served there. It's perfectly permissible to point one out to your waitress if you can't read the menu.

Red and white are usually used during celebrations. White rice is sometimes mixed with a special type of red bean to make *sekihan*, served during happy occasions such as special holidays or weddings. During unhappy times, such as during past Emperor Hirohito's illness before his death, *sekihan* is not eaten.

At the end of a meal, green tea is usually served. This is drunk very hot, without milk or sugar. Cups are usually filled only half to three-quarters full, as it may be too hot to hold a full cup. You may also see bits of tea leaves at the bottom. Incidentally, if a tea leaf or stem is standing up, it's considered very good luck.

In traditional Japanese restaurants, you will have a private *tatami* room for your party. And you'll often all be eating the same thing, so just expect your host to order for you. It's part of the group experience.

One last menu note: A *teishoku* is a complete meal (as opposed to à la carte) that includes a main dish, soup, rice, and pickles.

A Note on Fast Food

In the past two decades, fast food has become more common in Japan, with McDonald's and Kentucky Fried Chicken restaurants sprouting up everywhere. The proliferation of these eateries is so great many kids think they are a Japanese invention.

As fast food continues to become a part of the Japanese diet, etiquette rules adapt to keep pace with the change. Traditionally, you would never see a Japanese drinking or eating something while walking. As fast food becomes more popular, this practice is changing somewhat among the younger generation. However, older Japanese still find eating or drinking while walking to be offensive.

Picking Up the Tab

Who pays at a business meal is not dictated by any firm rule. However, if you feel you would like the meal to be your treat, you will probably have to be quick to grab the check before your intended guests do. Snatching the bill before someone else does is good etiquette, but the Japanese are quick and can make it difficult for you to pay. A way around this would be to invite your guests to an establishment you frequent and prearrange for the bill to be given directly to you.

If the other person has extended the dinner invitation to you, it's best to let him pay for it. You wouldn't want to inadvertently imply that he can't afford it.

The Japanese will not pore over a check—in fact, they may not look at it at all—for it will almost invariably be correct. (No tipping is required; see chapter 33.)

We've left out many Japanese foods: *sukiyaki, shabu shabu, kushi katsu,* among many others. With these, however, it will be easy enough to follow your host's lead. Play it safe and ask him to order for you if you're at all unsure of what's appropriate.

23
Gift-Giving

Gift-giving, a $92 billion industry in Japan, is an institutionalized custom. Gifts are thought to express one's true heart and to convey feelings such as gratitude and regret better than words. The gift-giving ritual was once very well defined and so important that one member of the family was made responsible for knowing what to give to whom, when, and how it should be wrapped. That is less the case today, though the custom remains a large part of business and social relations.

Traditionally, gifts are not opened in the presence of the giver, but this custom is sometimes forgone when it comes to Westerners. Your hosts, moreover, may very well expect you to open a gift when you receive it. If you do wish to open the gift and have asked if you may, do so carefully, respecting the packaging, as it is considered part of the present. If you don't open it, your hosts may tell you what the gift is. Don't be surprised, though, if a gift you've given is put aside unopened.

Gifts are presented humbly, often with comments like, "This is nothing at all," "A mere trifle," or "An item of no value." To give lavish gifts for display is considered gauche; as or more important than the price of the gift is its appropriateness and the care with which it was selected.

As a sign of respect, gifts are usually given and received with both hands. It is considered proper to thank a person when you receive a gift, before you part, and the next time you speak or write to him or her.

After receiving a gift, it is customary to return one (*o-kaeshi*) of a suitable value in the near future. The Japanese hate to leave the scales unbalanced. The price will depend upon the relationship and situation. (For example, the return gift custom for weddings, births, illnesses, and death is *hangaeshi:* about half the value of the gift received.) For this reason more than any other, the price of the gift should be in keeping with the occasion.

Gift-giving duties can create a heavy financial burden. Insurance companies have begun to offer hole-in-one golf insurance, as lucky golfers are obliged to send gifts to close friends, colleagues, and those who witnessed the event. A $10 policy covers as much as $2,000 worth of gifts and parties the fortunate golfer must provide for each hole-in-one.

Business Gifts

When it comes to business gifts, many of the humility rules are thrown out the window. Business gifts are purchased at prestigious department stores where they will be wrapped appropriately with the store's trademark paper. Although everyday products are the most common (whiskey, cooking oil, condiments, and other edibles, for example), only those in elaborate gift packages and elegant containers are given as presents. House plants, magazine subscriptions, and theater tickets are unusual but nevertheless interesting presents for people who may be getting many duplicates of the ordinary gifts. Since homes are small in Japan, gifts that can be consumed are considered the most practical.

It would be good form to take something from your home country with you on your visits to Japan. These should be items not readily or cheaply available in Japan. Beef, smoked meats, citrus fruits, expensive candy, and cheeses are always welcome gifts. Meat and fruits must first have been certified by your country's department of agriculture. Duty-free shops and other enterprises catering to Japanese tourists are good places to look for gifts as they will be packaged appropriately and might even be put on your flight for you.

Alcoholic beverages make good gifts to the Japanese. American spirits, such as bourbon, have a broad appeal, although something in a nice decanter is a more appropriate gift for a top executive. A bottle of alcohol can make a good group gift for members of the same department as often a department has its own stash for after-hours celebrations.

Other gift possibilities might be a special product of your company, leather goods, local crafts, Californian and European wines, items from famous places, famous brand items, and items from famous stores. Logo items designed to be useful in business can make good presents, but it's imperative that they be of high quality and it's better if they're made in your own country. A picture book of your state or a regional specialty or handicraft may help the recipient feel closer to you.

If you're giving an item made locally, look for something that symbolizes a desirable aspect of your relationship with the recipient: long objects (noodles were traditionally given to new neighbors to symbolize a long relationship), durable objects, nourishing objects, etc. Fans and objects with crane motifs are popular as symbols of good luck.

Sports-related items are usually well received, especially if it's a sport the receiver is interested in (golf is a pretty safe bet for Japanese businessmen). As you get to know the people you are dealing with, a more personal gift can be given—something for their hobby or special interest.

When giving individual gifts, be sure to have enough for each person present; if you don't, give all that you have to your contact and let him distribute them to the appropriate people. A corporate or group present is fine and may be more suitable for a first meeting.

If you are traveling to Japan, you should give your gifts toward the end of the first meeting of the day. Your Japanese hosts will usually give you something in return before you leave.

Keep a record of the gifts you receive and give, noting the ones that were especially well received by your Japanese counterparts.

Favors

It is considered rude to ask for a favor empty-handed, but these gifts should not be thought of as bribes. They should be in keeping with their name, *o-tsukai-mono* (something you can use). However, when dealing with Japanese who are aware that we don't have such elaborate gift-giving customs, it's best to make it clear that the present is in appreciation for the long relationship, lest they mistake it for boodle.

Midsummer and Year-End Gifts

Summer and year-end gift giving is such a long-established custom that for a Japanese to disregard these times would be a terrible breach of etiquette. Fortunately, these coincide with the biannual bonuses, so people have ready cash to buy them. *O-chūgen*, the midsummer gift custom, originated as consolation for the families of those who had died in the first half of the year. These days it involves everyone, though it still takes place during the two weeks before *o-bon* (mid-July in Tokyo, mid-August in some other regions), which is the holiday for honoring the dead.

O-seibo, the year-end gift giving, is even more widely observed than the midsummer custom as a token of gratitude for favors and loyalty. It is estimated that the Japanese spend $20 billion at *o-seibo* each year. Gifts are presented to friends and associates, superiors, teachers, benefactors, and anyone else to whom one feels indebted. Stores and companies often spend exorbitant sums of money to thank clients who have patronized them. Typical gifts consist of imported wine or fruit, tea or coffee sets, seaweed, dried goods, vegetable oil, specialty meats, whiskey, beer, *sake*, condiments, dairy products, or such things as blankets or towel sets. Businessmen usually give gifts costing an average of ¥ 10,000 (about $80), but the price will vary depending on the relationship with the recipient.

During the *o-chūgen* and *o-seibo* seasons, department stores open up special sections, sometimes a whole floor, to display their selection of typical gifts for these occasions. At these two times of year, department stores take orders and make thousands of deliveries. If you decide to participate, department stores are probably the best place for you to shop. This way the gift you buy won't be something unusable for the Japanese. More important, however, it will be packaged and wrapped properly and delivered, if you so choose.

Representatives from the major department stores will often visit corporate offices (and the homes of important clients) with glossy brochures describing the latest *o-chūgen* or *o-seibo* gifts. By placing their order with the sales rep or faxing it in, corporations save considerable gift-shopping time.

As many people receive numerous duplicates of the same items, unwanted gifts can be sold at a greatly reduced price to special stores that resell them to the public at a discount.

The gifts are most often delivered to the home address of the recipient. Individual department stores have their own fleet of trucks that deliver gifts in a timely manner.

People may keep a list of the gifts they receive and their value, which is useful in determining an appropriate gift for the next year. One may choose to send a gift back, if an undesired obligation comes with accepting it.

Congratulatory Gifts

Congratulatory occasions are birthdays (especially at sixty, seventy, seventy-seven, eighty-eight, and ninety-nine years of age), anniversaries, weddings, births, children's festivals, business openings, new homes, promotions, and such occasions as when a colleague's child graduates or passes college-entrance exams. Traditionally, fresh fish (usually red snapper since it's pronounced *tai* in Japanese and *medetai* means "auspicious") or dried bonito (*katsuo bushi*) were given at these times. These days congratulatory gifts are similar to those given at such times in the West. Money is given at weddings, which are exorbitant ceremonies in Japan. Crisp, newly minted ¥10,000 bills (¥20,000 is common) are placed in a proper envelope, which can be purchased at a stationery store. The amount a person gives varies from person to person, depending on the relationship with the bridal couple, and the envelope is placed on a special table in the wedding or reception hall.

When celebrating occasions such as weddings, corporate anniversaries, or the opening of a new business, the hosts usually present the guests with commemorative gifts or mementos.

Travel Gifts

Souvenirs (*o-miyage,*) are bought on trips for family, friends, and co-workers back home. Honeymoon couples often buy gifts to be presented as *o-kaeshi* upon their return. Fulfilling this obligation can take up so much of one's trip that many Japanese order from catalogues before they leave home. Thoughtful, inexpensive gifts are usually taken on a trip for people to whom one wants to express gratitude for some kindness.

New Year's Gifts

When calling on close friends and relatives to wish them a happy New Year, *o-toshi-dama* will usually be given to the children of the family. This is freshly printed money, *always* in the proper envelopes, one for each child. Before the guests leave, the receiving parents often secretly check the envelopes and give an appropriate amount per child to the visitors' children. The amount given depends on the relationship with the child's family and the child's age.

Get-Well Gifts

Calling on someone who is sick or who has had an accident is called *o-mimai*. On these occasions one may take flowers, fruit, or money, but potted plants have the connotation of being buried and the implication that the illness is firmly rooted. Presents are also given when someone recovers from a long illness or convalescence.

Gifts of Sympathy

When notified of a death, one should immediately pay a call to express one's sympathy. An offering of flowers, fruit, vegetables, incense or, as is most common, money should be brought. The amount given to the bereaved family is on average ¥10,000–¥20,000, but this differs from person to person, again depending on one's relationship with the deceased. Even people who are not very close to the departed may attend the funeral, and they may choose to give less.

Money Gifts

The Japanese consider unwrapped money to be coarse, so gifts of money are always given enclosed in paper. Special envelopes for special occasions may be purchased at almost any stationery store. It could be very offensive to use the wrong envelope, so make sure you obtain the proper one.

Envelopes and gifts are often inscribed with the person's name and appropriate sentiment. If you ask, the store will probably do it for you. Please note that while you can stamp your own seal with red ink, you should *never* write someone else's name in red, as it signals the end of a relationship. Long ago in China, names circled in red carried the death sentence.

Wrapping

The appearance of a gift is highly important. The container the gift comes in and its packaging are nearly as important as the contents. It is therefore essential that a gift be enclosed in a beautiful box or container wrapped properly. Japanese avoid using black or bold-colored wrapping paper. The black-and-white combination is reserved for funerals.

Because of the serious nature of a business gift, it is best to have gifts bought in a department store wrapped there in the paper appropriate to the occasion. A gift purchased and wrapped in a prestigious department store's paper adds to its value. As you may expect, a gift purchased from a supermarket and wrapped in their logo paper would not convey the proper image for a business gift. If you carry a gift to Japan, you can usually have your hotel wrap it for a fee.

What Not to Give

Superstitions die hard, so be aware: Gifts that consist of a number of items fewer than ten should be given in odd numbers (odd numbers are lucky as they represent the positive force of the universe). Tea sets, for example, usually come with five teacups, rather than four, as in the West. Four and nine are avoided on most occasions, as they have homonyms which mean "death" and "suffering," respectively. Hospitals in particular avoid these numbers.

Anything that cuts or could symbolize severing of a relationship should be avoided, such as scissors, knives, or letter openers. White handkerchiefs, reminiscent of sorrow, also indicate termination of a relationship.

Don't give anything that pictures the sixteen-petal chrysanthemum, as it is part of the Imperial Family's crest. Anything that depicts foxes, associated with fertility, or badgers, which are thought to be cunning, should also be avoided.

Flowers are usually reserved for courting, illnesses, and deaths (white and yellow chrysanthemums for funerals). If you do decide to take someone flowers, make sure you do not get the small bundles with lots of foliage used for altars or graves.

How Things Are Changing

Some stores have begun to discontinue their free gift-delivery service. Free delivery began as an incentive to lure customers and the practice became widespread, even for small purchases, at considerable cost to the stores. Supermarkets are leading the trend to charge customers a delivery fee, and there appears to be less resistance than expected on the part of consumers to pay for home-delivery services.

24
Visiting the
Japanese Home

By Western standards Japanese homes are very small. Apartments, especially in the city, are so diminutive that they are almost like closets. One-third of the housing in Tokyo averages only 121 square feet (11′ × 11′). When city dwellers are lucky enough to have a house and not just an apartment, any tiny bit of spare ground will have been turned into a miniature garden. Japanese rarely entertain in their homes because they do not consider their homes worthy of guests. If a foreigner expresses interest in visiting a Japanese home, however, an invitation might be forthcoming. Note that this is quite an exception to the rule and you should consider an invitation an honor.

Even if you never visit a Japanese home, you will probably at some point be invited to a traditional Japanese meal at a restaurant or inn. The etiquette for a home and a traditional restaurant is much the same.

Visiting Etiquette

Even before you ring the doorbell, you should remove any overcoat (coats used to be regarded as unclean, since they protect the wearer from the elements), as well as hat and gloves. If, however, you are just dropping in to say hello and your stay lasts only a few minutes, it is permissible to keep your coat on. Doing so also conveys to your host that your visit is intended to be brief. Regardless of the length of your stay, you should always remove your hat and gloves.

If there is no doorbell affixed to the outside of a house, you should not knock but slide the door open and call, *"Gomen kudasai"* (Please excuse me). Just inside the entry will be a small vestibule called a *genkan*. After being invited in, you must also remove your shoes, but take care not to turn your back on your host while you do it. Do not stand on the *genkan* floor in your stocking feet, but immediately step up into the house itself. When visiting a home, it is considered polite for you to then turn your shoes so the toes of your shoes point toward the door. (The hostess will do this for recalcitrants.)

It is customary to bring a properly wrapped gift when visiting someone. Some kind of food delicacy is common and should be presented immediately. If you are just visiting Japan, some memento from home would also be fine.

After removing your shoes (slip-on shoes can be a great asset), you will be given a one-size-fits-all-except-Westerners pair of slippers in which to walk down the hallways. As you pass the kitchen, be discreet and don't peek in. This is not a room the Japanese are proud of, so, out of courtesy, guests should keep their eyes straight ahead. If you need to use the rest room during your visit, be sure to change into the other set of slippers you will find there and, more importantly, be certain to leave them in the rest room when you leave.

When entering the house or any of the rooms, be careful not to put your fingers through the thin *shōji* paper sliding doors. Also, if you're tall, keep in mind that the doorways are only about six feet high. Remove your slippers before you enter the room, for only bare feet or socks may tread upon *tatami*. Make sure you have plenty of brand-new dark-colored socks (for women, extra hose) before you make your trip. Holes are not acceptable and you may not be able to buy any in Japan that will fit you.

The place nearest the *tokonoma* (alcove; see below) is reserved for the guest of honor. It's nice to not assume this is for you and wait for your host to insist you sit there. Incidentally, the best seat is with the back to the *tokonoma*. In the Japanese way of thinking, the important person should be framed by it, not looking at it.

You should kneel Japanese-style on the *tatami* mats, the proper way being with the knees a few inches apart and one big toe over the other. Your host will rescue you soon and insist that you sit comfortably. (Here the gesture of at least trying to sit properly is the point.) Comfortably means cross-legged for men in Western dress and with feet to the side for ladies. Wait for them to ask you to sit on the cushion.

Your Japanese hosts will not burden you with decisions about what you'd like—beer or tea, peanuts or sandwiches. They will simply serve you what they imagine you'd like.

Tatami

Tatami mats are three feet by six feet and made of tightly woven rice-straw pads about two inches thick. Rooms are built to contain a certain number of these three-by-six-foot mats, and the size of the room is referred to by the number of mats. A four-and-a-half-mat room, for example, would be nine feet by nine feet. A home will usually have at least two *tatami* mat rooms separated by sliding doors. These doors are covered with thick, opaque paper in the case of the doors called *fusuma*, or thinner rice paper pasted over a wood lattice door in the case of *shōji*. Either of these types of doors may be lifted out of their runners to make one large room. Remember, no shoes *or* slippers are worn on *tatami*.

A large *tatami* room is called a *zashiki*. These rooms traditionally have very little furniture, if any, or ornamentation on the walls. (Western homes, with adornment of every available wall space, are thought by the Japanese to look like museums.) The *zashiki* will, however, almost always have a *tokonoma,* an alcove usually containing a hanging scroll or a picture and a flower arrangement. By the way, the *tokonoma* is reserved for treasured items only and is not a place for personal articles, ashtrays, or beer glasses.

In the middle of the room will be a low table with cushions around it. In traditional homes, in winter a half *tatami* mat is often removed to expose a small chamber for hot coals in the floor under the table. This is called a *kotatsu*. The table is then usually replaced with one that has a removable top, allowing a quilt to be placed over it to contain the heat, so that one can dangle one's cold feet under the quilt and over the coals. With the modern *kotatsu,* however, the coals are dispensed with; the table is equipped with an electric heating element already attached under the table top.

As Western-style housing is becoming more prevalent, especially in urban areas, chances are good that, even if you are invited to a Japanese home, it will not be a traditional one. It may be furnished entirely in the Western style and there may be no *tatami* rooms. However, many of the same rules of etiquette still apply, such as taking a gift and removing shoes. Always follow your host's lead, and ask when you're in doubt.

Thank-You's

A few days after having been a guest at a Japanese home, you should thank the host or hostess via phone, letter, or a brief visit in which you express gratitude while standing in the entranceway. (Traditionally, if you enter the house, it becomes a formal visit, and tea and cakes must be served.)

25
The Tea Ceremony

In the course of doing business in Japan, you may be invited to a tea ceremony. This is a very kind invitation indeed; it's not extended to everyone. Regard it as a special honor and go prepared.

Once you accept an invitation, *do not cancel*. There is a saying that if you say you will attend, you must miss even your parent's funeral.

Practitioners of the tea ceremony learn their craft according to the traditions of one of the three main schools of tea. The ceremony described here is an example of Urasenke, one of the most popular schools.

There are many variations and different levels of formality to the tea ceremony, but the rules of conduct are basically the same.

Prepare yourself for the ceremony. Participants should dress in subdued colors. Avoid wearing perfume or jewelry (including a wristwatch) or anything that would disrupt the serene mood.

Traditionally, money is given to the host as a sign of gratitude and to help defray the cost of the ceremony. If you wish to follow this custom, give the money in an envelope (make sure you purchase the correct one) to the most senior guest, who will present it to the host. Another option would be to take the host a small gift, either an item from home or something you buy in Japan that reflects the simplicity of the ceremony. In such a case, leave the gift for the host in the waiting room, or give it to the most senior guest.

The Tea Room

Traditionally, the tea room is in a tea house situated in the garden of a private home or temple. Nowadays, however, they can also be found in large hotels and even in department stores.

The tea room is designed with harmony in mind—harmony of the kind that can be found only in the imperfection of nature. An amazing amount of money and care is expended to construct a humble and barren cottage from perfect materials to give the impression of refined simplicity.

Besides the tea room itself, there is a waiting room for the guests, a garden path connecting it to the tea room, and an anteroom for washing the utensils. The door into the tea room is small (less than three feet high) so that one must crawl through it; the intent is to humble high and low alike.

The Ceremony

Upon receiving an invitation to participate in a tea ceremony, call on the host or hostess about three days in advance to accept and to express thanks. Check to see what you need to bring (such as *kaishi*, a special paper tissue) and let them know if this is the first time you will be participating in a tea ceremony or if you are not familiar with their school's ceremony.

Fifteen or twenty minutes before the designated time, the guests will assemble in the waiting room. If the order is not predetermined, here they decide on the seating order, beginning with the eldest or highest ranking and ending with someone who is well versed in the ceremony.

The ceremony begins when the host enters the waiting room, bows silently, then retreats. Always return a bow made to you. Everything that happens from here on is rigidly set. The guests arrange themselves in the order that has been decided on. After changing into clean socks and leaving belongings in the waiting room, take the path through the garden to the tea room.

After cleansing your hands and rinsing your mouth in the provided basin, crawl silently through the entrance, turn and rearrange your shoes, and then move them out of the way.

Once in the tea room, a guest should go to the alcove, bow, admire the hanging scroll, and bow again. Approach and appreciate the brazier, then be seated out of the way. Seating—in the predetermined order, with the guest of honor sitting closest to the host—begins after the last person has entered.

When the host arrives, he or she will light incense in the charcoal and the main guest will ask on behalf of the others they be allowed to admire the incense case.

A meal of many small courses may follow. For this, adhere to the normal eating etiquette for a Japanese meal. Be sure to say *"osaki ni"* (see page 73) anytime you do anything before another guest. Take your cues for what to do from those around you. Sitting between two experienced guests can be very helpful for the newcomer.

When the meal is finished, the guests will retire to a Western-style room or arbor while the host prepares the tea utensils, tidies the room, and exchanges the scroll for a flower arrangement. When he (or she) is ready, he will sound a gong or appear and make another silent bow. The guests will then go through the ritual entrance again, this time admiring the flower arrangement. They will stop to look at the kettle, fire, and tea caddy before returning to their seats.

The host returns now and prepares a thick tea with practiced grace and precision of motion. This thick tea is passed from guest to guest in one big tea bowl. The ritual of drinking is to place the bowl on your left palm and steady it with your right hand. Then with a nod and an *"osaki ni"* to the next guest, turn the bowl twice clockwise so that the design is away from you.

You should take three and a half sips, then set the bowl down. Wipe the edge of the bowl where you drank with the *kaishi* you brought with you and turn the bowl back counterclockwise two times, so the design faces you again, and pass it to the next guest. Tea bowls are often delicate, low-fire ceramics and the host may therefore provide damp napkins in a separate bowl (instead of *kaishi*) for the guests to use.

When each guest has drunk from it, the bowl is returned to the host, who will pass it back to the guests to examine. The bowls are masterpieces of imperfection and usually have a history. Be sure to handle everything with two hands. The guests should also inquire about and examine carefully every other utensil that has been used.

Next, a thin tea is usually served along with little cakes. The atmosphere and procedure for this are very much relaxed. Guests are served in separate bowls this time but one at a time. You may sip this in any way you like, but be sure to drink the entire contents of the bowl this time. After drinking, wipe the place you drank from with your thumb and index finger and wipe your fingers on the *kaishi*.

When the utensils have been put away and the guests have expressed their gratitude, the ceremony is over. Three or four days later you should send a thank-you note to your host.

The tea ceremony described above is a common one but not by any means the only procedure. For example, a meal may not be served. Also, a ceremony performed by a master of a different school would vary somewhat. For example, in the other popular school, Omotesenke, the direction of the turning of the bowl and the number of times the bowl is wiped differs. However, the main procedures are similar.

This overview gives you an idea of how detailed and prescribed the ritual is. Be cautious about your conduct, but be relaxed and follow the lead of the other guests. In a tea ceremony, a guest can never make a mistake. Above all, don't fail to appreciate the simple, natural beauty of everything involved.

V

JAPANESE CORPORATE CULTURE

26
The Ways of a Traditional Japanese Company

How the operations of Japanese companies differ from those of companies in the West has been the subject of many recent books. Here, however, it's less important to suggest what the West might adopt from Japanese practices than to note how certain significant features influence Japanese dealings within the international business community. These features must be taken into account in any proposal by a Western interest that wishes to do business with the Japanese.

Lifetime Employment

It is a well-known tradition in Japan for large companies and government bureaus to employ workers for their entire working life. Actually, this affects only about a third of the work force, but it is generally the top third and is mostly male.

Large companies hire people right out of college into entry-level positions rather than as specialists. They will work in groups, carrying out group assignments under the supervision of a senior. They then move through an automatic system of promotions and pay raises until their forties, when discrepancies in promotions begin. For this reason, age and seniority are usually synonymous. The Japanese like the security this system offers, as they find it attracts dedicated workers.

Another type of automatic move within a company is the lateral move: through various departments and even other branch offices every two to five years. This exposes workers to a wide variety of experiences, allowing them to meet many different people and giving them an understanding of how their company functions as a whole. It also permits them to establish valuable contacts with workers in other departments, to whom they can later appeal for cooperation or assistance on projects or proposals.

Of course, not everyone is equal in skill or ambition. But the system of group work assignments and vague job descriptions permits those of greater skill within the group to compensate for those of lesser skill. This is true even if those of lesser skill are theoretically in charge.

Those who make it to the top in Japanese companies are people who have good interpersonal skills. This is because a top manager is more of a human-relations leader than a decision maker or a goal setter. Top managers in the Japanese system are good listeners and harmonizers. They know how to orchestrate the "right" environment and boost workers' morale. In keeping with the Japanese propensity for taking the long-term approach, they are measured much less on their quarterly or annual results than American managers are.

In the beginning, these managers-to-be are not promoted any more often than other employees, nor do they receive pay raises any faster. As their abilities become apparent, they are given tougher job assignments and put on an elite track that will move them properly through the right departments to prepare them for top management. From middle-level jobs on, differences in speed of promotion slowly begin to appear.

Japanese companies are ever conscious that their employees are their lifeblood. For this reason, business leaders tend to look after the physical needs and spiritual growth of their employees much as they would their own children.

One unique characteristic of the Japanese business world is the *keiretsu* corporate grouping of large, interlinked companies such as Mitsubishi, Mitsui, and Sumitomo. They usually include banking, manufacturing, real estate, and trading companies, as well as exclusive suppliers.

Making the "Company Man"

When a new group of recruits enters a company, typically on April 1, they are put through an extensive orientation, learning the corporate philosophy, motto, song, and so on, in a process that is also intended to initiate bonding between employees. To further the bonding process and the development of team spirit, events are scheduled throughout the year in which employees are expected to participate. These range from corporate group parties to a company sports competition, and numerous extracurricular clubs. Accordingly, a Japanese company sometimes seems like a social club as well as a business enterprise.

In most companies, employees receive extensive training throughout their career. When there is minimal likelihood the employee will leave the company, this is a good corporate investment. Service-industry and sales-position training includes instruction on the proper forms of etiquette to follow when answering the telephone, how to bow properly, and the correct way to exchange business cards.

Rather than laying off workers during recessionary periods, companies enlist the help of their employees in dealing with the problem. Fiscal measures are taken to protect all jobs, such as cutting salaries of top executives and deferring bonuses or pay raises until the company pulls out of the slump. For this reason, workers are not so worried about losing their jobs and are able to focus on the task at hand. Rather than letting the problem defeat morale, everyone pulls together and the work group usually emerges stronger, having endured the hardship together. This, of course, engenders a great deal of loyalty on behalf of the workers. In the event workers must be laid off, good companies consider it their responsibility to help their employees find another job and will ask other companies they have connections with, especially within their *keiretsu*, to assist them.

The Work Group

Most assignments are carried out by work groups of about ten to fifteen workers. The group (*ka*) is headed by a chief called the *kachō*—usually someone around forty years of age who has been with the company for at least fifteen years. Individual roles and assignments for accomplishing a project are not well defined within the group. Each group member does whatever is necessary in the way of tasks to complete the project.

During the three to four years a worker may spend in one group before he is rotated into another, that group becomes the focus of his life. He will spend from forty-five to fifty-five hours each week working closely on projects with other group members, with whom he will also spend much of his social life. As always, maintaining harmony in all relationships has major importance.

Harmony is stressed in Japan, to be sure, but this is primarily at the surface level. As one Japanese scientist working in the United States has described, American companies are like a zoo at feeding time, where all the animals openly fend for themselves and go for the food. Japanese companies, he says, are more like an arboretum where the plants are apparently living together in peaceful harmony above ground, but the unseen roots below the surface are in continual competition, fighting each other for survival.

Project Teams

When special problems arise, project teams consisting of managers and employees from various departments are created, much like a task force. At meetings, team members "feel out" one another, hearing everyone's opinion until a consensus is reached. The conclusion is then written up in a *ringi-sho* (proposal) that is circulated around the group and then up through the hierarchy for approval.

If the team is initiated by someone in middle or lower management, the meetings often take place informally, sometimes even after work hours.

The "Organic" System

One of the salient differences between Japanese and Western companies is the formalized structure the Japanese have for a "from-bottom-then-upward" method of making proposals and participating in decisions. While the ultimate authority for approving all important and far-reaching measures does of course lie at the top, by and large the system is an "organic" one.

In essence, this organic system means that all levels of company management are involved in the process of proposal initiation and final decision making. One good point about the system is that, in typical companies, in the end no single person must take sole responsibility for a mistake or a bad decision. And all share in the success of the enterprise. There has been a complete consensus about the matter throughout the group, from bottom to top as from top to bottom.

There are, of course, a number of companies that use a more top-down management style. As this is important information to you, it is one of the aspects of a potential trading partner you should research. Companies that give individuals more decision-making power can make decisions faster but can also drop a project more easily. Those that use a consensus style take longer to get serious, but once they do they are unlikely to drop it.

Kaizen

Continuous improvement in the workplace, a process known as *kaizen,* is characteristic of many Japanese companies. Workers are brought into the process through soliciting their suggestions. Improvements suggested by the workers help the company's morale by building greater team spirit and contribute to the financial success by increasing efficiency of output. In American businesses, improvements are generally made in spurts, and suggestions by employees, as well as instances of their adoption, are few. Japanese companies that practice *kaizen,* however, find that through constant attention they experience a more steady improvement and have a more committed workforce.

The Personal Side of Business

The personal side of Japanese business is of no mean consequence. Much energy is expended on creating and maintaining the relationships upon which companies will depend for many years.

To the Japanese way of thinking, business is more a commitment than a simple transaction. Personal relationships are vital, therefore, in developing the humanistic and emotional ties that ensure a business relationship will not end as soon as it becomes less profitable for one party, the way Western business connections often do. Business relationships based on an impersonal profitability are not the Japanese way.

Accordingly, dropping by regularly or calling just to say hello is a common courtesy in Japan. Small gifts are given at special times and attention is paid to a person's hobbies or particular interests. (Gift giving is discussed more thoroughly in chapter 23.)

Japanese manufacturers go to great lengths to convince everyone important to them—wholesaler, retailer, and consumer—of their commitment to the human aspects of business. This concern should be even more critical in the case of a foreign producer selling products in Japan. In the past, many foreign companies have used the Japanese market for the spot sale of goods, earning a much-deserved and not well-regarded "here today, gone tomorrow" reputation.

Subcontractors

The relationship between companies, subcontractors, and suppliers in Japan is generally a strong one. Manufacturers give suppliers advice on how to improve the quality and production of the components they produce, and the suppliers benefit by having a steady buyer. In the case of small *keiretsu* subcontractors, they often produce for one company only.

About 70 percent of a Nissan car is made from *keiretsu* parts, while the typical GM car has only 40 percent of the parts made by a subcontractor. When times are good the Japanese subcontractors sometimes up their prices with the excuse that items are scarce due to strong demand. When times get tough, however, the large manufacturers are able to pressure their suppliers to lower prices, enabling the purchasing company to stay more competitive.

The Detail Man's Role

A very important public arm of a Japanese manufacturer is its detail force, sales representatives who establish close relationships with both the wholesaler and the retailer.

These sales reps may visit retailers a couple of times a month, often with the wholesaler's representative. They will solicit frank opinions from both regarding the product in question and its future. They will also offer the retailer merchandising assistance, including suggestions on store layouts and product displays.

For the same purpose, an overseas firm dealing with trading companies in Japan would be well served by setting up a liaison office to represent its interests there. People in this office will be helpful in establishing those critical personal relationships. They can gather market response on products, collect information on new competition, and keep an eye on how well the trading company and wholesaler are handling a product's distribution.

The staff of a branch or large liaison office should not be all Japanese. Keeping some expatriates involved is a sign of commitment to the enterprise in Japan. More important than business experience for these people, though, is some expertise in the Japanese language and some knowledge of Japanese customs. While most of the running of the business may be better left to competent Japanese nationals, the Japanese-speaking foreigners could offer symbolic assurances of commitment to the Japanese market and provide the close contact the Japanese are accustomed to.

27
The "New Breeds"

The Japanese work environment is undergoing change. As the "old guard" retires, younger Japanese, with a perspective that often differs radically from their predecessors, are increasingly taking the helm. While there are great internal as well as external pressures to change, only time will tell how far these modifications will go.

The New Woman

Female office workers fall into one of two categories. Those referred to as *ippan-shoku* include support staff such as "office ladies" (see chapter 16). *Sōgō-shoku*, on the other hand, are career-track women who are given the same responsibilities and opportunities as men. Involved in company decision making, they are treated in much the same way as their male counterparts.

A labor shortage, combined with the world's longest life span and lowest birth rate, has recently forced companies to hire women in managerial positions. In 1988, women still accounted for only 1.29 percent of all corporate managers, but in a survey by the *Japan Economic Journal* of 1,000 companies, 41 percent had women in managerial positions, albeit at the lower levels.

Japanese women are at a turning point. Economics and societal pressure no longer dictate that a woman must be married by a certain age nor that she automatically quit her job once she marries. A recent survey has shown that only 20 percent of young women wish to become full-time housewives.

Marketing, advertising, publishing, and entertainment are industries where women have an easier time making inroads, and especially in these areas you may encounter highly successful female entrepreneurs.

The Fluid Workforce

Work attitudes of the younger generations also vary somewhat from their superiors. Job switching and mid-life career changes, once thought of as futile and a sign of disloyalty, are becoming more common. Increasingly, young Japanese are willing to sacrifice career security for higher pay or greater choice in their career path. This has given rise to a growing headhunting industry.

Some of the more progressive companies are responding with selection systems that allow employees to apply for certain placements within the company. This is in contrast to the traditional method of assigning employees to a particular department.

Working with a Younger Generation

While older Japanese still wield the greatest power in most companies, more authority is beginning to be commanded by a younger generation led by baby boomers now in their forties (Japanese born after World War II), who grew up in a time of growth and increasing affluence, contrasted with their parents and grandparents who made many sacrifices and endured Draconian circumstances during and following the war. The vast difference in experience accounts in part for the dissimilar attitudes toward work, the family, and leisure, which vary greatly from generation to generation and from person to person.

The younger generations have grown up in a time of great wealth. Many have rejected the formality of traditional culture and are viewed by older generations as bored and greedy for material wealth. They are sometimes referred to as *shinjinrui* by their elders. Although this literally means "new breed," it can have a negative connotation.

Among this group you can see a large change in clothing: Italian cut olive- and earth-tone suits with discreetly striped shirts and fashionable ties are common attire for new employees, especially in Tokyo. Owning a car has become a popular status symbol, and dating is much more open. Groups of young people get together for road trips. Younger males seem to take a more publicly active role in pursuing girlfriends, who for their part are often looking for boyfriends who are charming and have a cosmopolitan image. Many in this age group have been influenced by travel or homestays abroad.

Japanese in their teens exhibit even less traditional behavior. Acquisition of material things and the pursuit of pleasure and leisure time are their main interests. With the advent of video games, they spend much time alone, causing their families to worry about their general lack of social relationships.

Younger Japanese workers are choosing to spend more time with their families and are pushing for more leisure time in which they can enjoy themselves, develop a new skill, or pursue a hobby. You may also find that younger Japanese are more inclined to invite guests to their homes and have dinner parties that include both husbands and wives.

Returnees

In the past three decades, the number of company employees who have been sent abroad on foreign work assignments has increased significantly. They often return to their home country discouraged to find that their colleagues have shut them out. Being out of the mainstream for so long can make successful reentry a difficult proposition. But even worse, as a result of living in a foreign, extroverted society the returnees are sometimes seen as a threat to the company's harmony.

The returnees naturally add an international edge to their company's corporate culture, and, as the number of returnees grows, so will their influence. The most forward-looking companies value the fresh perspective and ideas.

About 10,000 *kikoku shijo* (children of returnees) attempt to readapt to Japanese society each year. Fitting back in to their own society and school culture can be extremely challenging. Lacking familiarity with their peers' norms, and sometimes with a limited ability to communicate in Japanese, they are often harassed by other kids. When a *kikoku shijo* commits an illegal act, the media often portrays it as a result of living abroad, aggravating the image of these children as a negative influence. Presently, about 600 international schools and a few colleges try to accommodate the *kikoku shijo*'s particular needs.

Japanese society is beginning to accept the *kikoku shijo* to a degree, and some companies are actually seeking them out (though many still see them as selfish individualists who lack corporate loyalty). It is hoped their experiences overseas will contribute to the development of a more creative workforce. Those who have a difficult time fitting back into society tend to work for foreign companies and move in circles outside the Japanese mainstream.

The New Emerging Attitudes

In the past few years, Japan has become one of the world's top economic powers. The Japanese are adjusting to this with a mixture of pride and trepidation. With the new role comes new responsibilities and sometimes unwelcome expectations from other members of the world community. Messages often seem mixed: We chastise them for taking a passive role in some matters and get indignant when they are too assertive in others.

For their part, the Japanese are responding with mixed behavior, ranging from becoming "more Japanese" to becoming aggressive and arrogant. It is an interesting time of transition. Just as the Japanese despised the condescending attitude of Western nations, these countries are now having to face their own music.

28
Working for a Japanese Company— in Japan

If you go to work for a Japanese company in Japan, your job is going to be full of fresh challenges that will be both exciting and frustrating. Whether you're a manager or part of the staff, you'll find that your Japanese colleagues have a remarkable capacity for ambiguity and uncertainty.

One of your first complaints will probably be the lack of a job description. In fact, it may be quite some time before you have any idea what it is you are supposed to be doing. Your job may include many other duties than what you might expect from your title. The fact that you may have signed a contract to do a specific job is irrelevant. Patience is advised.

Another area where ambiguity and vagueness prevail is in decision making. It may bother you to find that no one will lay his cards on the table. Such apparent uncertainty, however, is necessary for the proper unfolding of the all-important consensus. If each person reveals his position, he will feel compelled to defend and stick to his stand, creating a win-or-lose situation.

Harmony and "face" are maintained by a subtle feeling out of the other's position, often one on one before the group meets. Vagueness is esteemed and directness is equated with arrogance.

The Japanese work in an open office environment, with very few private offices. This seems to be predicated on the belief that maintaining group closeness is essential to harmony. People who do not want to join the group are perceived as selfish—something akin to reading a book in a corner at a party. It's this loyalty to the group that has given Japanese establishments their excellent reputation for service. To perform in a less than desirable way would be letting down the group, although this may very well feel suffocating to the individualistic Westerner.

The openness of the work environment is conducive to good communication, as contact between superiors and colleagues is maximized. Japanese feel that having a separate office isolates you from the informal flow of information that is so critical in their system. The office layout illustrated (page 170) is typical of many large corporations and government offices.

Don't expect your work day necessarily to end at the scheduled time. Most Japanese office workers don't leave before their boss does; if their boss leaves early, they often stay much later. If you encounter this situation and find yourself obligated to do the same, it does no good to get out the rule book. You'll just embarrass your boss, and he'll be more convinced than ever that foreigners can't understand Japanese ways.

There is generally a change in the atmosphere of the office after closing time. The most productive meetings, in fact, often occur after hours. Employees tend to tell more jokes and behave much more informally after "official" business hours, even though they continue to work.

Salary and Bonuses

Depending on the industry, your salary in Japan may be equal to or higher than one an employee in the West would receive for comparable work and responsibility. Despite higher pay, however, you will probably find you have less discretionary income, as the cost of living is considerably higher in Japan. You may be compelled to live without certain luxuries that we take for granted in the West.

If the company makes a profit, there is the benefit of bonuses. Bonuses are given twice a year, in early summer and the big one at the end of the year. It is, in effect, a profit-sharing plan. The bonus

TYPICAL OFFICE LAYOUT

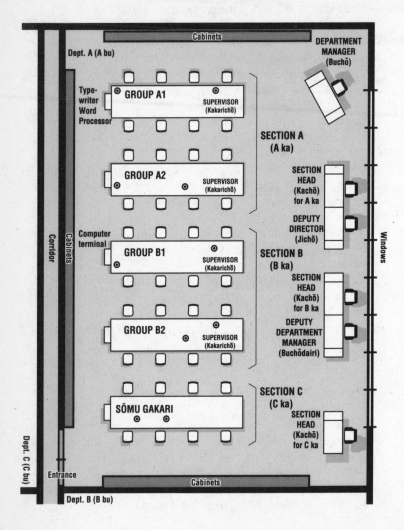

an employee receives can be quite substantial. Depending on one's rank, rating, and how the company is faring, an employee's bonus usually ranges from two to six month's pay, but can be larger. Of course, bonuses will be smaller in bad times, but all of this is yet another example of the sense of group and group effort and the need, therefore, to make a substantial contribution to the group.

Workaholism

Most Westerners consider work to be primarily a means to a financial end. Aside from certain workaholics, most Westerners seem to center their lives around family and friends, not around the work environment.

Japanese workers, on the other hand, don't perceive work as a form of punishment. Indeed, business life is often preferred to home life. A dedication to work that is uncommon in the West seems more the rule than the exception. Consequently, if you refuse to work overtime or if you ask for time off for routine family affairs, you won't create a very good impression. If you decline to go on group trips or drinking outings with co-workers, you'll undermine the solidarity of the work group.

This is not to say that the Japanese are intransigent about such matters or that to work for a Japanese company is to indenture yourself to it. This is only to say that these customs apply and any deviation from them behooves you to acquit yourself in some compensatory fashion.

Concern in recent years has been building about how the stress of overwork is affecting the health of Japan's workforce. *Karōshi* (death from overwork) is the term most widely used to explain a new phenomenon. Those who refuse to work overtime or who take a sick day or a vacation fear that their jobs may be at risk. The typical victim is a male, white-collar worker in his forties or fifties. Victims' groups estimate 10,000 *karōshi* deaths per year, but the Ministry of Labor denies that such a large problem exists. A labor law was revised in 1988 in an effort to decrease the 48-hour work week to 40 hours. While the law resulted in some temporary relief, a year later employees of only 9.6 percent of firms were working the new 40-hour week.

Meetings

To keep everyone informed and to get a feeling for others' opinions, meetings are held with great frequency in Japan. They are usually opened by the highest-level person present but will then be chaired by the person who initiated it, even if he or she is in a relatively low-level position.

What Not to Do

If you have a good idea, don't be impromptu and bring it up in a meeting. Rather, suggest it to someone who has influence, such as your superior or an influential colleague, who can pass the idea along. If you spring something on everyone in a meeting, your idea will probably be pushed aside. Also, be forewarned that ideas generated by an individual become group ideas. The idea's originator becomes long forgotten. Here's a list of other caveats:

- Don't expect your private affairs to be nobody else's business. Remember that this is a group of tight solidarity.
- Don't slap your co-workers on the back in easy familiarity.
- Don't defend yourself when reprimanded. Your colleagues will assume that your intentions were right, even if you acted in error. Simply apologize and accept the criticism.
- Don't press a colleague or boss to make a decision in public. Don't corner him with, "Would you sign here, please."
- Don't laugh at a Japanese to his face, even if you think he should recognize that you're laughing with him.
- Don't joke around at work. In Japan there is a time and place for everything. While a congenial atmosphere is important, much of the usual joke telling that goes on in Western companies is out of place on the job in Japan.
- Don't ask for a private office.

The following diagrams portray appropriate seating arrangements within a Japanese company.

MEETING SEATING PROTOCOL

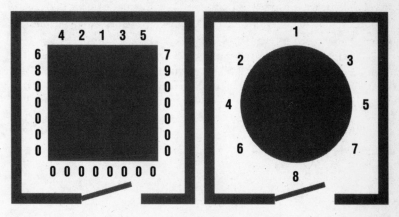

INTERDEPARTMENTAL

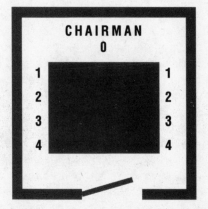

Elevator Etiquette

Although elevator etiquette is not as commonly or strictly observed as it was in the past, you may find yourself in a situation where you don't want to appear presumptuous in front of your boss or an important client. In that case you may wish you knew the conventions older Japanese were accustomed to.

The rear left (as you enter) was traditionally reserved for the most important person. If all the occupants are of similar status, this corner will often remain vacant as no one wants to appear as though they are presuming to be above the others. If there is no attendant to run the elevator, the lowest-level person works the controls. When an elevator door opens, lower-level personnel who have been waiting will sometimes not enter if it is occupied by important people.

As a Manager

When choosing a good manager, Americans tend to value rational skills, while Japanese prize interpersonal skills. If you're a manager in a Japanese company, you'll be spending 90 percent of your time listening and the other 10 percent talking, not the other way around.

In group meetings, listen to everyone else's opinion before expressing yours. You'll notice how the Japanese avoid open disagreement with one another. When dissension is necessary, they preface their remarks with buffer phrases such as, "I concur but ..." or "I agree in principle ..." If you think the group is being manipulated by one person, you can shelve the subject with this handy phrase: *Kangaemashō* (Let's think about it).

As a manager, you may have to modify the ways in which you are used to communicating with others. Don't send out a lot of memos and ask for memos in return. The Japanese don't regard this type of written correspondence as a valid means of communication except to share pertinent information. They will, however, pay a lot of attention to what you say. Don't be surprised when people want to discuss points of view with you in private prior to a group meeting.

The best decision in the West is the one that brings the best results. In Japan it's the one everyone can agree on. To exercise your influence in a subtle fashion and to help the group come to a consensus, it will be necessary to spend time with individuals outside the work environment—at lunch, at dinner, or, most commonly, over a drink. If you ever need to request personal help, it is best done in this way as well.

You will need to take a more personal interest in your workers in Japan than you probably would in your own country. Japanese workers usually won't volunteer information about their problems to you, but they will expect you to inquire regularly.

Among the values foreign managers have said they learned from their work experience in Japan are patience, tolerance, tact, flexibility, sensitivity, thoughtfulness, and a live-and-let-live attitude. You will need these very qualities to get the most from your experience in Japan.

Allow yourself plenty of time to adapt to your new role—it may take at least a year. Remaining flexible will be your greatest asset in encountering the unfamiliar situations ahead of you. Keep in the front of your mind the Japanese successes and the amazing efficiency with which the Japanese way functions when the whole problem is considered. It will help you to be less judgmental when little differences appear.

At a company party, Japanese managers have been known to slip away early, after having made financial arrangements for the party to continue. The reasoning is that the party can be more relaxed without the manager there, thus freeing both manager and employees from prescribed roles. If you're a foreign manager in a Japanese company, you might want to do the same.

As a Lower-Level Worker

While working for a Japanese company, it is only natural to modify your behavior in order to work more effectively with your Japanese colleagues. At the same time, however, you will wish to retain key facets of your personality and Western cultural values. This is not always easy and will require compromise on your part as well as from those who work with you.

Remember that advancement will probably be slower in a Japanese company and that respect and responsibility are earned. Many foreigners agree that it takes showing a substantial commitment, such as working in a company for more than three years, to earn colleagues' and superiors' trust. It may take at least this long before you become privy to information of real value.

If at any time you feel you are being treated unfairly, you may feel compelled to point this out to your boss. Be respectful, be gently forthright, and don't be obnoxious. Probably a one-on-one approach at an informal time would be best. Let him know that you can't be fully productive when your needs aren't being met. If the subject is touchy, get someone to act as a go-between for you. Having a mentor to intercede for you and help you in promotions is extremely beneficial.

Keep in mind, though, that while in the United States there is the saying "The squeaky wheel gets oiled," the Japanese have an equally popular saying: "The nail that sticks up gets hit."

Greater Benefits

There are many frustrations in working in Japan, but there will also be great benefits to your career. View your career in larger, longer terms. Opportunities for learning and new experiences will be innumerable, to say nothing of individual growth. If you're easily discouraged or if you want only what's tried and familiar, you'd do better to stay home.

As international business makes the world seem smaller and smaller, companies and executives who don't have a global picture will find themselves left behind. If you've had experience working in another culture, especially one as successful at business as Japan, your worth will be more highly prized.

29
Working for a Japanese Company— in the West

If you are one of the more than 300,000 people working for a Japanese company located in North America, you're bound to find an East–West blend in the way things are done. The other chapters in this section should give you at least some idea where, for your company, East begins and West ends. But anticipate rough spots— especially in your own mind—that will need to be smoothed out.

The number of Japanese managers in your company, and where they are positioned in the organizational structure, will greatly affect how much of a Japanese flavor the company will have. This organizational structure will be determined by the nature of the industry involved. A sales-oriented business, such as the automobile industry, will usually employ more local personnel because contact with customers is a primary activity. A trading company, on the other hand, tends to employ more Japanese because good communication with the home office is essential.

Some Useful Character Traits

Before we discuss some of the issues you may be confronted with, it would be helpful to familiarize yourself with some of the qualities the Japanese value in employees.

Diligence and persistence: One of the most admirable qualities in the eyes of the Japanese is an ability to persist, even when the gains seem extremely small. In their minds, the *gambaru* spirit, which enables one to "hang in" and do one's best regardless of the situation, is one of the major ingredients for success. The saying *"Ishi no ue nimo sannen"* means that sitting on a rock for three years heats it up, implying that perseverance brings success.

Perceptiveness and sensitivity to subtlety: Inherent in the Japanese language is a tendency toward vagueness and subtlety. Because of this, it is critical that you learn to read between the lines. If you're not able to understand what is being implied, you'll miss the major points of the conversation and will probably be seen as rather dense. As a consequence, you may be given less and less responsibility and information of importance.

Flexibility and cooperation: The Japanese group orientation does not mean that employees become like worker ants, mindlessly working like cogs on a wheel. It does, however, require individuals to become team players and harmonize with the group. This is one reason flexibility is so important. Cookie-cutter employees are ineffectual in institutions where job descriptions are vague and where each is expected to do whatever is necessary to get the job done. This doesn't mean giving up individual uniqueness and homogenizing, but rather finding a way to blend and harmonize the individual pattern with the group pattern. It takes everyone cooperating to make the greatest achievements. And because of the value placed on internal harmony, it is also important not to be overtly or aggressively competitive or to attempt to be perceived as better.

Diplomacy: In a land where loss of face leads to loss of self-respect, an ability to be diplomatic is a definite asset. It requires a respect for all rules—even unwritten rules—and a sensitivity to what may cause embarrassment. Whereas challenging the rules may be viewed as positive in the United States, predictability is important in the Japanese company. Unpredictable people cannot be trusted, and Japanese counterparts and superiors may tire of wondering what you will do next.

Frustrations

If your main motivation for working for a Japanese company in the West has to do with trying something new and different that might benefit you in the long run, you're not likely to be disappointed. But if you think working for a Japanese company will mean quick advancement, you're working for the wrong company. Promotion in a Japanese company comes slowly. It's the way things work.

Westerners will find as well—at least it's been a common complaint of Westerners—that they are essentially barred from promotion to top positions. The Japanese response to this is that few foreigners take the time to learn the Japanese language, which they feel is important for top-level communication. This is a valid point. It's hard to imagine an American company in Japan employing non-English speakers in its highest posts. Also, finding a Japanese mentor is a key to making your way to the higher echelons in management.

Another frustration is that Japanese managers are usually rotated out just when one has gotten to know them. As mentioned before, Japanese companies do this to give their employees a well-rounded background in all aspects of their company. It would behoove you to continue to foster a good relationship even after your manager has returned to Japan. Take advantage of the situation, if you can, by making him your connection to the home office. And remember, these contacts become more and more valuable as the person moves up in the company's hierarchy.

Working for a Japanese Manager

It's possible that many little things your Japanese manager does will be misunderstood if you interpret them in terms of your own sense of propriety. Try to be clear on which aspects of a person's behavior are a product of cultural mores before judging too harshly. For example, you may have a manager who seems not to care or who seems aloof because he doesn't relate in the casual and outgoing manner you're accustomed to. You're aware that reserve is a valued characteristic in Japan. But you may be surprised when he actually shows more interest in your personal problems than a Western manager would or when he returns from a trip home with personal little presents for everyone in the office.

Consider what would be expected of a Japanese in your position, even though you may not choose to affect that behavior. Japanese assistant managers, for example, act much like faithful retainers. They will not leave work until their boss does. If their superior is out or at a meeting, the assistant will not even go to lunch until the manager returns. Be aware of such notions your manager may have brought with him to the West.

Loyalty is one of them. If you try to make your Japanese boss look good by giving him credit for things you've done, it will eventually pay off with large dividends later. Learn also how to negate without saying no.

It's possible that the Japanese employees in your company always have lunch together, as though it were some kind of law. This may seem silly or ethnocentric to you, but keep in mind that Americans and other foreign nationals in Japan do the same thing. Any penetration of the group barrier is beneficial. Informal interaction, such as during lunch or after hours, is very important. But go slowly. Shows of friendliness that are too enthusiastic are not regarded favorably.

What to Expect from Evaluations

The frequency and method of evaluation will vary from company to company and depend additionally upon your position. Rather than just looking at results, supervisors usually consider aspects of the process as well, such as trying hard and showing improvement. One major Japanese corporation evaluates managers once a year and lower-level employees twice a year. Lower-lever personnel are evaluated on the following factors: quality of work, quantity of work, job knowledge, attendance, and cooperation. The manager or supervisor submits to personnel a written report with a 1-to-5 rating. The rating is based on a curve with 10 percent receiving a 5, 15 percent a 4, 50 percent a 3, 15 percent a 2, and 10 percent a 1. Supervisors in the same company are rated on: results related to the corporate goals, job knowledge, organizing ability, dependability, and interpersonal skills.

A verbal evaluation may surprise you with its candor. Japanese superiors take their role as mentors very seriously and often act like Zen masters with a disciple, giving "spiritual," unachievable goals.

Receiving this sort of "guidance" (criticism) from a superior in Japan is considered a compliment. If he didn't think you had potential, he probably wouldn't bother to try to inspire you to do better by being hard on you.

Japanese tend to expect workers at all levels to make more of a positive contribution than companies in the West. Finding ways to improve quality or process are looked upon very favorably. You will be seen in a better light, however, if you appear to be contributing out of a desire to be involved rather than for personal credit.

The more you appear to be committed to long-term employment, the more training you are likely to receive. It's not as important to appear to be the smartest as it is to appear to try hard, to be self-motivated, and to be eager to learn.

Don't forget how important detail is to the Japanese. They expect thoroughness in all areas and, of course, no less in information. Hard data—specific numbers or details—will be required much more often than in American companies.

You will probably get less direction from a Japanese boss. Instructions and expectations may not be made clear. He will expect you to take a great deal of initiative and figure out for yourself what needs to be done. It is also unlikely that you will get the on-going positive feedback for jobs well done that you are accustomed to. Japanese adults know by subtleties that their efforts are appreciated and could very well find the "strokes" given in an American company to be patronizing.

Visiting the Home Office

A company trip to Japan will offer you some unique opportunities. You will have an advantage over other travelers because you are already "in" to a degree, because you work for the same company as many of the Japanese you will meet. For general purposes, however, you are still an outsider, like all foreigners, and you will be treated unfailingly as a guest.

The "office ladies"—whose job, among other things, is to prepare tea and coffee for the men—will probably wait on you hand and foot (whether you're male or female, your guest status requires this treatment). Don't assume, however, that you can feel free to make menial requests of any female there. Asking someone to do an inappropriate job is as rude in Japan as it is elsewhere. The answer, though, is not to make your own coffee; you will probably have a young male assigned to take care of you and you can let your needs be known to him.

Women in Japanese Companies

Overall, your situation as a woman in a Japanese company may be difficult if your goals include large financial rewards or an honest-to-goodness senior title that is not for "face" only. Again, if your primary motivation is less goal-directed than experience-related, satisfaction won't be hard to find.

If you are the only female at, say, the managerial level, you may find yourself rather isolated in the corporate world. Because of your gender you may come up against many walls, and hopefully these will not be insurmountable. Keep in mind too, however, that while assertiveness has helped many women in American corporations, it can work against you in Japan. It will be important that you don't step on people's toes.

If you are an executive secretary or administrative assistant to a Japanese man, you may have to "train" your boss in how and how not to utilize you. In Japan there are few people in such roles. Women primarily do clerical work. Therefore, your boss may unwittingly make inappropriate requests, such as for photocopying or tea making, even if that is someone else's job. Unaggressively help him to understand your role.

Benefits

A friend of mine who works for a major Japanese trading company feels that his greatest benefit is the on-the-job training. Being trained as a generalist in a large, diversified company gives one experience and knowledge that isn't ordinarily available, even in an MBA program. Others say the experience gives them security.

The primary advantage, however, is the opportunity to get exposure to another culture. These days, an aspiring business person cannot afford not to be international. For that matter, it will soon be necessary for everyone to have some intercultural experience to break down prejudices, identify stereotyping, and give Westerners perspective on their own cultural limitations. Without the tools to deal with this, we may find that as the world shrinks, the abysses between the cultures seem to grow greater.

VI

THE "OTHER JAPAN"

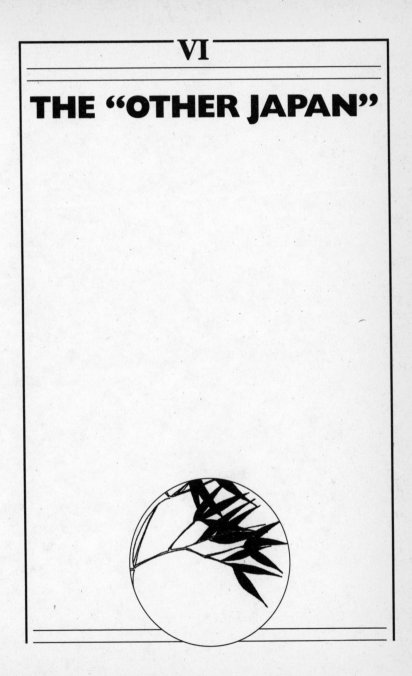

30
Out on One's Own

With business in Japan finished for the day, you may want to do some exploring about town on your own. In play as in work, Japan differs a great deal from the West, so if you're adventurous there's much that can be interesting or fun. Don't enter a place without *some* awareness ahead of time, however; if you're totally unprepared, it could turn into a costly, if not embarrassing, evening.

Coffee Shops

Coffee shops (*kissaten*) are everywhere. They are the most popular, most casual of the common meeting places. These coffee shops offer a selection of coffees from numerous countries, and some offer alcoholic beverages as well as a modest menu. The coffee is ground fresh and prepared before you; it has a wonderful rich flavor, but by American standards it is strong and expensive and does not come with free refills.

Some *kissaten* turn into what is called *sunakku* (snack shops) at night and stay open all hours. These are distinguishable by the bottles of whiskey visible behind the bar.

Since there are so many *kissaten*, many develop features to make them unique and cater to a specific crowd. They may specialize in a particular kind of music, such as jazz, classical, or rock; some are furnished with unusual decor or a distinctive theme (a period in history or a foreign land); some have underdressed or stylishly dressed waitresses; others are geared toward businessmen, featuring a coin-operated fax machine and financial newspapers.

Some *kissaten* encourage single foreigners to give their Japanese patrons an opportunity to practice English, and others simply give foreigners a chance to meet one another. These are sometimes called "conversation lounges." For specific names and locations, pick up a copy of *Tokyo Journal* or *Osaka Time Out*, English-language magazines that can be purchased at bookstores, hotels, airports, and numerous other places catering to foreigners. Conversation lounges can also be places to find someone to go dancing with, since many discos expect people to come as couples.

Drinking Establishments

There are hundreds of thousands of night spots in Tokyo alone. They range from local pubs to *karaoke* singing bars (see chapter 21) to high-class cabarets and nightclubs, including clubs with exclusively male hosts catering to women and clubs that feature only Caucasian hostesses. In Tokyo, the best and most expensive of these nightspots are found in the Ginza. The Akasaka, Shinjuku, Shibuya, and Ikebukuro districts have lots of fine, more moderately priced places; Asakusa has less-expensive places. Roppongi is fairly new as an entertainment district and attracts a younger, more international clientele.

At many clubs it is understood that hostesses come with the drinks. If you do not request a particular hostess, the next in line will be assigned to you—often one for each person at the table, but sometimes more and sometimes fewer.

These hostesses act as modern-day *geisha* (professional entertainers), pouring drinks for the men, smiling, listening, teasing, and in general getting everyone to loosen up. The patron is expected to buy drinks for these hostesses, but in addition he is charged by the hour for each hostess's time. The hostess may be called away to another table and then end up playing a version of musical tables. You, of course, are required to pay the basic fee for each one who shares a bit of her company with you.

A well-known customer will be granted "signing privileges" in lieu of on-the-spot payment. Having this privilege in a number of expensive clubs is a must for properly impressing business clients.

One may have to pay more if a hostess is requested by name. This often translates into improved service—though service is almost always good—and in the presence of others gives one status.

A *nomiya* is something like a neighborhood pub. There are no hostesses, although some *nomiya* have women tending bar who will join customers if they're not busy. Many *nomiya* have a red lantern out front and are thus called *akachōchin*. (Do not confuse this with a Western style "red light" district.) These establishments tend not to be expensive, but if there are no prices posted in the window or on a placard outside, it may indicate otherwise.

Whether at a nightclub or a *nomiya,* one can buy a bottle of scotch or brandy, write one's name on it, and have it kept there. In fact, it is somewhat of a status symbol to have bottles at a number of exclusive clubs. Each time you visit these places, your bottle will be produced, along with glasses, ice, little bottles of water, and snacks. There is a fee for the service and the snacks.

Watch Your Wallet

Unlike in many countries, "watching your wallet" in Japan does not mean you need to fear being robbed. Japan is one of the safest countries in the world. The Japanese, in fact, will knock themselves out trying to return a wallet you left in a bar, taxi, or train. So the warning here applies to certain establishments that have absolutely astronomical prices (such as $200 or $300 for a scotch and soda). You must be careful you don't naively wander into such places.

The reason why they can get away with charging such exorbitant prices is that many businessmen are on very generous expense accounts and are eager to use up their allotted amount so that it isn't cut back the following month. The government used to allow these extravagant expense accounts as tax write-offs because it assumed that much entertaining must take place before relationships are cemented. The tax laws have been made more stringent, but the custom remains.

In addition to the already outrageous prices, many establishments will tack little charges on the bills of nonregular guests. It's best to go with a well-known customer. The Japanese themselves rarely walk in "cold" off the street.

Checking out a club before you go in could indeed save you a lot of money and some embarrassment.

31
Love and Sex
in Japan

The Japanese attitude toward sex is quite matter-of-fact and not laden with the same overtones of morality as in the West, especially where Puritan influence is strong. In Japan, sex is simply considered one of the more pleasurable necessities of life. In one clean sweep, this attitude removes many of the taboos Westerners have grown accustomed to when it comes to sex.

Sex in Japan is also not as strongly associated with love as it is in Western culture; it's seen as having more to do with desire. While sex fulfills certain urges and marriage fulfills the obligation to perpetuate the family name, love is often viewed as the cause of pain and heartache—the stuff of which fantasy is made in novels, movies, and comics. This is not to imply, however, that love is not an important part of the modern marriage.

Traditionally, marriages were contracted into. They were to fulfill duty—and were not to be the only means of satisfying sexual needs. Extramarital relationships, therefore, escaped moral censorship. But, as with everything, there has been a double standard. As long as a man had the wherewithal to do so, he was perfectly free to keep a mistress (or two) or to seek sexual pleasure any way he chose. A mistress, in fact, contributed to his esteem. Women, however, were expected to toe the line of marriage. Many of these attitudes persist today.

Geisha

When Westerners think of Japan, often they think of *geisha*—mannered women in whiteface, wig, and formal kimono. *Geisha* (pronounced gay-sha) translates literally as "one who is versed in the arts." A *geisha* works as a hostess and entertainer for small parties or for individuals. She pours *sake*, sings, dances, plays classical musical instruments, and gets her clients to enjoy themselves by engaging them in witty conversation, and by teasing and playing games. The cost to the customer for an evening at a restaurant where *geisha* entertain is exceedingly high. Such *geisha* houses are not marked and may not be entered without an introduction. Consider yourself very lucky if you are taken to such a traditional place of entertainment, even though you may find it all incomprehensible, if not downright boring.

The *geisha* makes money for herself in the form of tips (this being one of the few instances in which a tip is appropriate), but this money is usually reserved for the purchase of kimono. The actual fees for the evening's entertainment are paid to the *geisha* house.

Geisha are not prostitutes. Most have lovers or patrons who help to look after their welfare. Sleeping with the men they entertain is not as frequent or as important as the *geisha*'s role in breaking down the hard shell of Japanese reserve and in performing classical music and dance.

Originally *geisha* often came from poor families who needed to "sell" their daughters in order to survive. Upon signing a contract, parents or guardians were given a sum of money that was calculated based on the length of indenture and the girl's personal attributes. Today, young girls enter the *geisha* profession of their own free will.

A girl enters a *geisha* house by her early teens and spends many hard years of apprenticeship, not only attending lessons in music and dance but doing physical labor as well. By her mid-teens she is a half-*geisha* and can accompany older *geisha* to parties at restaurants where they will entertain. After a few more years of apprenticeship and an examination given by the *geisha* headquarters, the girl's house madam, and her music teachers, the girl becomes a full-fledged *geisha*.

Today the *geisha* profession has greatly declined, since much of their function has been taken over by bar hostesses. What these hostesses in nightclubs and cabarets have to offer instead is less personal and less traditional but comparatively cheaper Western-style entertainment.

Bar Hostesses

There are estimated to be well over half a million bar hostesses in Japan. As with *geisha*, it would be erroneous to assume that they are prostitutes (although, of course, some of them are). Many are married or living with a boyfriend, while others just simply "aren't that kind of woman," even though their job requires they give the impression they are. The fact of the matter is that the job pays very well—better than most jobs a woman in Japan can find. This is all the more so for the many Philippine and Thai women who now compete in the entertainment industry.

The club or hostess will sometimes accept the liability of a customer's bill, in effect giving him credit privileges. A hostess may choose to do this because she can tack on a substantial extra fee for allowing the privilege. Securing that money, however, would then be her responsibility, and sometimes the club will insist that she deposit a large sum of her own money before she can bestow such a privilege on a customer.

There are plenty of hostesses, though, who are willing to sell their pleasures and still others who would honestly opt to spend more time with a man because they like him. (If you want a date with one of these women, you might offer to escort her to a restaurant or meet her at a nearby late-night *kissaten* directly after she gets off work.)

One breach of etiquette that foreigners frequently commit is to bring these newfound liaisons to social events connected with business or business associates. This is not to be done.

Gay Life

Homosexuality in Japan doesn't carry the stigma it does in the West, even as homosexuals in Japan are not "out" as they are in large American cities. In Tokyo there are numerous gay bars in the Shinjuku 2-chome area to the east of Gyoen Ōdōri. As well as catering to gay men and women, a number of these bars also cater to the heterosexual clientele. As kind of a theme, there are some bars with gay men in drag that businessmen and office ladies frequent for an entertaining evening or as a trendy place to go.

Gay bars are much smaller in Japan than in the West; discos are few. It depends, of course, on the establishment, but foreigners will find most of these places friendly and pleasant. For details, check with the Tokyo Gay Support Group listed in the *Tokyo Journal*.

Many Japanese men are slender and sensitive by nature. Do not assume they are homosexual just by their appearance.

Love Hotels

A popular place for lovers is something called a love hotel (*tsurekomi hoteru* or *rabu hoteru*). The charge is calculated by the hour or by the night, and the rooms are decorated to satisfy the wildest fantasies imaginable (including rocket-ship beds and basketball hoops). Of course, some are just typical hotels, or traditional *ryokan,* but the rooms in even these will often come equipped with rows of mirrors or closed-circuit television and almost all provide condoms. There are literally tens of thousands of these love hotels in Tokyo alone.

Soapland

From 1193 to 1956 prostitution was legal, licensed, and immensely popular in Japan. When it was banned, much of it simply went underground, usually "fronting" as a Turkish bathhouse (*toruko*). Due to a protest from the Turkish embassy, Turkish baths now officially have a new name—Soapland. Not all *sōpurando* allow foreigners, although some cater to them and there are a few expressly for women. The largest in the world is in Osaka. It has a total of ten floors and includes a cabaret, a garden bath, and a bath for women only.

The law requires that there be a window on each door but does not specify where. Therefore, they're usually situated in a place that offers no view, or else a towel is conveniently placed over them. Separate payments are made to enter the establishment and to the person rendering the service.

32
Baths and Spas

Baths—very hot baths—are a trademark of Japan. They are part of Japanese family life, social life, and recreation. Baths are for cleansing, soaking, relaxing—and, on occasion, talking business. Even in modern Japan, the tradition of bathing continues in the home and at hot springs and spas.

Hot Springs and Spas

One asset of Japan many foreigners are unfamiliar with is hot springs (*onsen*). Throughout Japan there are 13,300 hot springs, many of which are mineral baths with medicinal properties.

In most of these, great pains have been taken to give the impression you are bathing outdoors in a serene natural setting (at some places you might actually be outdoors). Large windows look out to lovely landscaping or the landscaping may be indoors, the bath having been built around massive boulders complete with grotto and ferns.

Many inns, known as *ryokan*, are located near or around these hot springs. *Ryokan* are in the traditional Japanese style, with *tatami* floors, sliding doors, and meals served in the room. If you have the time and the inclination, a trip out of the city to a hot springs and *ryokan* will prove more than worth your while. The whole atmosphere of the place—rather a world unto itself—is something you won't experience anywhere else.

Bathing Etiquette

Whether you're at a *ryokan* or someone's home (in which case the only difference is that you'll be alone), bathing etiquette is the same. At an inn, you will probably be shown to the bath soon after arriving, if it's toward evening. This is a wonderful way to cleanse your body of the dirt and fatigue of the trip and begin your stay with a fresh spirit. At someone's home, the bath will be prepared and you as a guest will be offered the bath first.

Hot springs and public baths are communal, although almost all these days are segregated by the sexes. You will be given a small hand towel for the triple purpose of washing, drying, and protecting your modesty. When not in the bath, this is to be draped discreetly over the pubic region (forget the rest of you, women, as this is all that really counts). In all baths, because others will be using the same water to bathe in, *soap is never to be taken into a bath.*

Upon entering the bathing room, you will find a bucket or plastic tub. With water from the bath or a faucet along the wall, dump a few bucketfuls over yourself. Although theoretically you're supposed to wash before soaking, most Japanese will get into the bath at this point. The water temperature ranges from 105 degrees to 110 degrees Fahrenheit, so get in quickly—or slowly, if that's the only way you can do it—and keep still. Moving about makes the water feel hotter.

When you do wash, you must do so outside the tub. Again, use water from the faucet or from the tub to fill your bucket with clear water; soap up your towel and wash with it. Rinse your soapy hand in this bucket of clear water and then empty the water out before dipping the bucket into the bath to refill. Use plenty of scoops of water to get off all the soap. Now you can relax in the tub once again.

Perhaps you've noticed when drying your car that a damp cloth works better than a dry one. This applies to the human body as well. Once again, your miraculous little hand towel is there to do the job. Just make sure you wring it out well before you leave the bathing area.

If you're in a home, do *not* let the water out of the bath once you're done. The bath is to be used by the entire household.

Ryokan Etiquette

At a Japanese-style inn, you will find your room to be a basic, typically Japanese *tatami* room (or *zashiki*). There will be no furniture other than the low table in the center of the floor and probably nothing on the walls. The architecture of the room itself captures a simple natural beauty. There will be no locks on the sliding doors to your room, and you needn't concern yourself about it. You'll be surprised to find yourself feeling comfortable, secure, and private in this room. For the period of your stay, it will serve as parlor, dining room, and bedroom for you. *Do not wear shoes or slippers in it.*

Somewhere in your room you will find a light cotton kimono called a *yukata.* In most places, this is to be worn only in the confines of your room for relaxing and sleeping. At a hot-springs resort, however, you may wear it anywhere: strolling, dining, or even to a movie. Be sure that the left lapel crosses over the right; the right crossing over the left symbolizes mourning. The *yukata* in your room is not to be taken with you as a souvenir. They can usually be purchased close by.

Breakfast and dinner (excluding beverages) are usually included in your room charge. The meals will be served in your room on large lacquered trays brought up to you by the *ryokan* attendant. Most inns are aware that foreigners prefer what they're accustomed to over the Japanese breakfast of soup, fish, and rice. If that is indeed what you want, speak to the front desk and ask for *yōshoku,* Western food. A Japanese dinner (*washoku,* or Japanese food) is always to be recommended. There may be an extra fee for *yōshoku,* and most likely it won't be as good.

At night, the table will be set aside by the *ryokan* attendant and bedding will be taken from a closet. These pads or mattresses, called *futon,* are very comfortable. The only thing you might find unaccommodating is the pillow. Rather than feathers, it's filled with buckwheat chaff and feels something like an overstuffed bean bag. There's usually a cushion in the room that you can appropriate to your purposes.

Tips may be given in *ryokan.* It is customary to give two or three thousand yen beforehand to the person who will be looking after you. This is the person who brings the tea after you have been shown your room (often not the same as the person who shows you your room). Just hand it to her as she is about to leave after serving the tea, bow slightly, and mumble something like *osewa ni narimasu* (thank you for your assistance).

33
Incidentals

Hotels

Hotels in Japan are not much different from hotels everywhere except that the Japanese predilection for paying attention to detail is ever apparent.

You will often find a small refrigerator in your room stocked with a variety of beverages and snacks. Usually this works on the honor system, and it is your responsibility to record your daily consumption on the forms provided on top of the refrigerator. (At some hotels, your consumption will be registered at the front desk by way of remote control. Inventory is taken in the morning, during which time the refrigerator becomes locked shut. Therefore, do not use the refrigerator to store your own purchases from the outside, like a cup of yogurt for breakfast, unless you think you will be able to beat the clock.) Take these forms with you when you check out. A 10 to 15 percent service charge is added to your bill at most hotels. This takes the place of tipping, which is not customary in Japan.

In addition to the numerous luxurious and high-priced accommodations, there are also reasonably priced business hotels (not to be confused with love hotels—see chapter 31). Capsule hotels are literally just big enough to sleep and sit in. They come with a television set and a few other amenities and are very inexpensive. There are reasonably priced *ryokan* (Japanese-style inns) and wildly expensive ones.

The Japan National Tourist Organization (JNTO) will send you the *Japan Hotel Guide* and *Japan Ryokan Guide* free of charge. These list prices and other helpful information. (For the JNTO office nearest you, refer to appendix C.) For the cheapest accommodations when visiting the countryside, ask them about *minshuku*, which is lodging at a private house. European-style "pensions" usually include a Western-style breakfast and dinner in the price. They are also cheaper than hotels in resort areas but provide no towels or toiletries.

Tipping

There is virtually no tipping in Japan. It can, in fact, cause some Japanese to become indignant, as pride is taken in doing one's job well for the sheer service of it. (An elderly professor told me that when he came to the United States in his youth, his first job was as a delivery boy for a pharmacy. After making his first delivery in the hilly terrain of San Francisco, the kindly customer called after him and tossed him a dime. The young man caught the dime, but then realizing it was money, threw it back at the customer. It was his last delivery.)

If you feel particularly grateful to a maid or someone else, a small gift would be appropriate—or just a sincere expression of thanks, especially in Japanese. A service charge is usually added to hotel and some restaurant bills, but, in any case, no further gratuity is either expected or wanted.

Traditionally "tea money" (*chadai*) was given to the proprietors on one's arrival at or departure from an inn. This money, shared among the servants, was enclosed in a proper envelope called *shūgi bukuro* or at least wrapped in white paper. (See chapter 32 for the present-day custom.) In the same way a tip may be given to a translator or someone else who has performed extensive service for you.

Umbrellas

Japan is a country that enjoys abundant rainfall, but the moisture can sometimes be a nuisance when trying to navigate down a busy

Tokyo sidewalk with an umbrella. Be sure to leave your wet umbrella in one of the stands located outside the entrances of stores and businesses or use one of the plastic bags provided for this purpose.

Toilets

The truly traditional Japanese toilet is a "squatter," basically a hole over an open pit with an absolutely lethal smell. The updated version is porcelain and may or may not flush. The end you are meant to face usually has a flared protector. (A friend of mine discovered after two years in Japan that she'd been facing the wrong direction all along, when she and other members of her household were discussing why she had put a poster on the wall you didn't face!)

Toilets and baths are in separate rooms, so be sure to ask for the toilet and not a bathroom. Frequently a home will also have a urinal nestling a few naphthalene balls to combat the smell. Ladies, don't despair if you're shown to the urinal. There will be another door inside leading to the toilet stall. Knock on the door to see if it's occupied; if so, you will hear a knock back.

Western-style toilets are gradually becoming commonplace, though many Japanese express an aversion to putting their skin on something other people have sat on. These toilets, being in an unheated part of the house, will sometimes have a heated seat or a terry-cloth seat sock to take the chill off.

On many toilets you can have your choice of flushes by pushing the handle toward the 大 mark for a big flush and to the 小 for a small one. Many toilets in homes have a water spout and sink on the top where the water runs before filling the tank. Used for washing your hands in, it is a way of conserving water as well as space.

Places that cater to foreigners will often have both a Japanese- and a Western-style toilet. In the event that you've forgotten how to use a Western one, there will frequently be diagrams depicting the correct method.

In many public places, there will be only one rest room for both men and women. Sometimes two separate doors—one for men and one for women—will lead into a common rest room for use by both.

(I can remember the first time I popped into one of these. Finding myself among a number of urinating men, I promptly exited, convinced I had my Japanese characters for men and women mixed up.) Even restaurants and bars frequently have just one room with a couple of urinals and stalls to be shared by all. It's all handled very matter-of-factly.

Electricity

Japan uses 100 volts, A.C., although many hotels have 110- and 220-volt outlets to accommodate Western appliances. Electricity is 50 cycles in the eastern part of Japan (Tokyo) and 60 cycles in the western part (Osaka, Kyoto, and Nagoya). Appliances made for 60 cycles will run more slowly in Tokyo; those set for 50 cycles will run more quickly (and therefore get hotter) in Osaka. This means you could damage or burn out the motor in your appliance unless there is "50/60 hertz" written on it.

Banks, Checks, and Credit Cards

Bank hours are 9:00 A.M. to 3:00 P.M. Monday through Friday. Their Automatic Teller Machines are open until 7:00 P.M. on weekdays and 9 A.M. to 5 P.M. on Saturday and Sunday. Personal checks are not accepted anywhere. Traveler's checks, however, are taken at major banks, hotels, some *ryokan*, and large stores in the larger cities. International credit cards are also accepted at major establishments. Some branches of some Japanese banks provide foreign staff to help foreign customers. Citibank has many branches and is by far the best equipped for efficient transfer of funds and other multicurrency services.

If you have a debit card from a major American bank that is part of a network (Star, Cirrus, Plus) you can withdraw funds from your American account while in Japan for a small fee. Contact your network for locations of ATM's in Japan. Many are conveniently located in downtown areas and in major Japanese department stores.

Shopping

Typical quality souvenirs from Japan include pearls, silks, watches, radios, cameras, cloisonné, lacquerware, pottery, wood-block prints, chinaware, dolls, fans, and paper lanterns.

Small shops off the beaten track tend to have more flavor, but many of the items mentioned above may be purchased tax-free at designated stores. You will find tax-free shops in airports, near or in your hotel, and in some of the large underground shopping malls. You will need to present your passport and keep the documentation they give you.

Department stores usually close around six o'clock in the evening and are often closed on one weekday. Many, such as Isetan and Seibu, have a foreign customer-service desk and provide discounts, parking, free museum tickets, and other conveniences to foreigners who register there. Haggling is not done in these or other fixed-price stores, though bargaining is sometimes done in a subtle fashion in art, antiques, and tourist shops, and in electronics stores.

For electronic items, the Akihabara area of Tokyo is the place to go. There are literally thousands of shops, large and small, and they are very competitive. Look for tax-free signs. One can bargain at stores in Akihabara.

The Ginza is a very colorful and lively district full of large and small stores alike, selling all kinds of merchandise.

Available free of charge from the Japan National Tourist Organization is a directory of stores, listed by the merchandise they carry, called *Souvenirs of Japan*.

Mass Media

National and international news can be found in one of the many English-language daily newspapers: the *Japan Times, Daily Yomiuri, Mainichi Daily News,* and *Asahi Evening News*. The *Nikkei Weekly* and *Asian Wall Street Journal* provide good business news; they can be found at bookstores where English language books are sold. The *Financial Times of London* and the *International Herald Tribune* are printed locally and available for daily delivery.

Some news programs and most English-language movies are also broadcast in English. These days most television sets are manufactured with bilingual capabilities. By pushing the bilingual button, you can choose to hear these programs in either Japanese, English, or both (English coming out of one speaker and Japanese out of the other). Check English language newspapers for information on which programs are bilingual.

For useful local magazines in English that feature articles of interest and entertainment listings, as well as information on local festivals, see appendix G.

Post Offices

Post office hours are from 9:00 A.M. to 5:00 P.M. Monday through Friday. Main post offices are open on Saturdays from 9:00 A.M. until between 12:30 and 5:00 P.M., depending on the size. The Tokyo Central Post Office is open seven days a week: 9:00 A.M. to 7:00 P.M. Monday through Friday, 9:00 A.M. to 5:00 P.M. Saturday, and 9:00 A.M. to 12:30 P.M. Sundays and holidays. The Central Post Office number is (03) 3284-9593.

34
Living in Japan

I f you are going to Japan to live, the first thing to deal with when taking up residence is culture shock. Your ability to deal with this will determine how much enjoyment you will get out of your first six months, the critical ones.

Adjusting to any foreign culture is not easy, but adapting to one as different as Japan's can be a problem. One recommendation of psychologists is to make friends, both Japanese and foreign, as soon as possible. Your Japanese friends will help you understand why things are done the way they are. Your foreign friends will help you to see how the adjustment is made and offer you a release for pent-up reactions. If you work, take time to socialize with your fellow workers after hours. Wives who don't work can meet people by taking up a traditional art form or some other cultural study.

Do something to alleviate stress every day. Jog, meditate, or walk through a park. Local sports clubs run by the ward or city government offer very cheap yet well-equipped facilities for swimming, weight training, and many other sports activities.

Try to learn Japanese as soon as you can. Take classes before you go, if possible. If not, enroll in classes as soon as you arrive. Communication will make your stay more comfortable and rewarding. Learning the language will improve your relationships with Japanese so your friendships will not be limited to other foreigners and Japanese who speak English.

Another piece of advice is to get out of your environment once a month. Living in a large, overpopulated city, such as Tokyo, can be a stressful experience; you may begin to feel closed in. Take a day or two to go someplace out in the country, perhaps a hot spring or at least to another town. Japan has a great number of beautiful and historical destinations where life moves at a slower pace. Don't miss the opportunity to experience some of the varied and unique flavors of the more remote places. Mountains are close by for hiking, and you can check the *Tokyo Weekender* (a free English-language paper) for events in town and local festivals.

If you have brought your whole family with you to Japan, it is important to make time to communicate regularly with other family members about how you are feeling. Problems can be avoided or minimized if they are caught early enough. One family member may be perfectly content in the new environment, while another may feel threatened, confused, or depressed. Be sure to set aside a time each day or week when you can discuss problems, experiences, and new issues.

Be prepared to feel different and possibly discriminated against because you are in a minority. Being a foreigner has its advantages as well as disadvantages, and the sense of being foreign is liable to be stronger in such a homogeneous society. Avoid the urge to feel angry and frustrated when things are slow or seem absurd. It's good to take stock regularly of why you are there. It is certainly not wise to complain or to be critical. Remember that things will seem confusing when cultural and language barriers exist. When this happens, it's easy to assume that the behavior of others is irregular. If you truly believe that you can make a constructive complaint, or that you have noticed some potentially dangerous situation that has been overlooked, be sure to begin your statement with an apology and to frame what you have to say in polite language. Otherwise you are most likely to be ignored.

There are centers that provide workshops on adaptation skills. Advertisements for these can sometimes be seen in the *Tokyo Journal*. See appendix B for some useful telephone numbers to help you through the more difficult times.

Housing

Finding living quarters anywhere in Japan is not an easy task, but it's most difficult in Tokyo. Rents are high, especially if you want to avoid a long (and usually horrendous) morning commute.

In your search for a place to live, you will probably come across the term "mansion" (*manshon*). These are simply more deluxe and expensive quarters than the tiny rooms Japanese call "apartments" (*apāto*); "mansions" are often privately owned, like condominiums.

Your best method of search will probably be through ads in English-language newspapers, the *Tokyo Journal*, the *Tokyo Weekender*, and through your acquaintances. Foreigners frequently turn their apartments over to other foreigners when they leave. Your Japanese acquaintances might know someone who knows someone who could give you an important introduction.

Try not to be offended if a landlord refuses to rent to you. Foreigners are short-term tenants who usually don't know the customs or the language.

Be prepared to pay a handsome deposit fee. This *shikikin,* or *hoshōkin,* is returned to you when you leave. However, *kenrikin* ("key money," sometimes called *reikin,* "thank-you money") is not refundable; it's a gift to the landlord. The general rule is that to move into an apartment or house in Tokyo, you should be prepared to put out about five times your monthly rent (two months' rent for *shikikin,* one month's rent for *reikin,* another month's rent to the rental agent if you use one, plus the first month's rent). Only a portion of this will be returned when you leave.

When paying rent (or lesson fees or anything else of that nature), be sure to put the money in an envelope. Your landlord (or teacher) may provide you with one to be reused each month. If he or she does not, you may purchase one for this specific purpose; in the event that you don't have one, any envelope will do. If the landlord does not live nearby, rent may be paid through the local bank; rental agents can provide you with details on this.

Japanese companies usually provide subsidized housing or low-interest loans for employees. If you are working for a Japanese company in Japan, you employer will probably help you with your housing arrangements.

The typical Japanese house does not come with many of the amenities we take for granted in the United States, such as wall-to-wall carpeting and central heating. In addition, most Japanese do not have clothes dryers or dishwashers.

Foreign Wives in Japan

If you are a Western woman living in or visiting Japan with your husband or boyfriend, it will be easier on you if you are aware of the cultural differences that affect you. If your husband is working with the Japanese, your understanding and acceptance of the customs in Japan will greatly contribute to your husband's success and your own ease.

The main area in which you will feel the difference is entertainment. Your husband will be requested and expected to "go out with the boys" frequently, and it will be necessary that he do so to establish close relationships. Although with younger people there are more couples entertaining, most older Japanese males are more comfortable with just the men.

If you are living in Japan, establish your own circle of friends or get to know the wives of your husband's colleagues. There are also many support groups for foreign wives. See the *Tokyo Journal* or *Tokyo Weekender*.

If you invite your husband's Japanese associate and his wife to your home, don't be surprised if the wife doesn't come if it's an older, more traditional couple. If she does come, it would be Japanese-like of you to invite her to join you in the kitchen and spend your own time there when not serving. Younger couples, however, entertain more in the Western tradition.

If you are just visiting Japan with your husband, sign up for tours and other things to occupy your time. Maybe one of the Japanese wives or female office workers can accompany you shopping. Understand that the demands put on your husband will be different from in the West. Be prepared for the custom of "men first."

Coming Prepared

The only way to soften the blow of adapting to a foreign culture is to prepare yourself as much as possible. Along with language training, try to get as much education on the customs as you can. Take advantage of the many good books available (see appendix F). Be prepared to ride trains, buses, and subways, or even purchase a bicycle or scooter. These are all convenient ways of getting around in congested cities where parking is a major problem.

Familiarizing yourself with the food ahead of time is not a major problem these days. Most Western cities have an ample variety of Japanese restaurants, and it would be wise to acquaint yourself with them before arriving in Japan.

Japanese medicines, which are usually unlabeled and in powdered form, take some getting used to. You may be grateful for a stash of over-the-counter remedies brought with you from your own country (although a few, Sudafed, for example, may be prohibited). Medicine, in general, seems one area in which Japan is behind. And while there are a great many good doctors in Japan, their "bedside manner" may not be what you're used to. For example, they normally are not prepared to discuss an ailment with the patient.

Once you get to Japan, you may find that household items that are relatively inexpensive at home, such as plastic trash cans, are expensive. Pack as much as you can in reusable plastic or rubber containers, especially if your company is footing the bill for shipping but not for new purchases. Your shipments (both air and sea) may arrive late, so be prepared.

When times do get hard, don't forget to look to others for help. Every other expatriate before you has had to go through the adjustment and can relate, in varying degrees, to what you're experiencing. Then, too, don't forget to prepare yourself for the culture shock of returning home, which may be much worse.

35
The Greeting Card and Other Rituals

An important part of Japanese life is to regularly thank those to whom one feels indebted. Twice a year, cards are sent: one is a summer greeting and the other is a wish for a prosperous New Year. The purpose of these cards is to convey to the receivers that you are thinking of them and wish to continue your good relationship.

As discussed in chapter 23, *o-chūgen* and *o-seibo* are the biggest gift-giving seasons. One is also expected to send cards called *shochū-mimai* or *zansho-mimai* and *nengajō* during these two gift-giving seasons.

Summer Greeting

About the middle of July, the rainy season begins to wind down and Japan becomes unbearably hot and humid. Near the end of the month, it is common to show concern for one's friends, neighbors, and business associates, by sending out *shochū-mimai* cards (usually postcard-type). These are greetings that inquire about the person's health and depict a cool or calming scene to give you a sense of relief from the heat. They often begin with a comment about how hot it is and how the sender hopes the receiver is staying healthy despite the oppressive heat and humidity. These can be purchased at many stationery stores and department stores.

New Year's Cards

More prevalent than the summer greeting card is the *nengajō,* a card to be sent at year's end. Because everyone sends *nengajō* the post office usually hires temporary mail carriers to deliver the stacks of cards to households and businesses. Like *shochū-mimai, nengajō* can be bought at a variety of shops. Cards usually come with a preprinted message, congratulating the recipients on the beginning of the new year and thanking them for favors done during the previous year. There's usually room for writing a personal comment, although many people simply stamp it with their seal, and they often depict the animal from the Chinese zodiac that corresponds to the coming year.

The cards are mailed before the end of the year, but since they shouldn't be received before New Year's Day, the post office usually holds all *nengajō* until the first, when they are delivered in bunches to each address. Since most people send a large number of these cards at one time, it is most convenient to tie them in a bundle and take them directly to the post office.

The greeting expressed at this time both verbally and on the card is *Shinen askemashite omedetō gozaimasu,* literally "Congratulations on the opening of the New Year." Consequently, it is never said before January first.

If you wish to send a Western New Year's card or summer greeting, send a Japanese translation along with it, so the recipient may understand your message. Nonreligious "Season's Greetings" Christmas cards may be used either as a Christmas greeting (if that's your custom) or a New Year's greeting. If you choose to send a New Year's greeting from the United States, mail it so it arrives after New Year's Day and not before.

Visiting

In addition to the New Year's and mid-year festivities, there are other occasions when personal calls should be made. These are for such purposes as inquiring after an accident or illness (*o-mimai*), for offering congratulations on auspicious occasions, and when one moves into a new neighborhood. In this last instance, the new person should visit his neighbors on both sides and the three across the street. Buckwheat noodles, being long and thin, were traditionally given to new neighbors, symbolizing the desire for the acquaintance-ship to be long, even if it is "thin." (This is also a pun, as *soba* means both "noodles" and "nearby.") Nowadays, gifts are likely to be more modern, if they are given at all. If you are the recipient of any of the above visits, return visits should be paid to express thanks with *Sen-jitsu wa dōmo arigatō gozaimashita* (Thank you for the other day).

At the above times, you should expect just to stand in the en-tranceway, because once a guest enters the house, it becomes a social call. If you are invited in, however, you should not overstay your welcome because polite Japanese will always try to make you feel that you should stay longer. If your host or hostess insists that you stay, you should insist that they not see you to the door, though they will do so. Bow as you leave the room and again in the vestibule as you say thank you and good-bye.

Japanese are known to say, as Westerners might, "Stop by when-ever you're in the area" or "We're always home on Sundays—stop by anytime." In most cases, these are just polite words and are not to be taken seriously. On the other hand, sometimes you'll find that they will stop in because they were in the neighborhood. If someone visits without calling first, you are under less obligation to entertain and feed them properly.

Weddings and Funerals

Should you be invited to a wedding or funeral, see chapter 23 for the proper gift to take and be sure to wear appropriate clothing. A black formal suit is the most appropriate attire for men on both occasions, with a black tie for funerals and a white tie for weddings. Women wear kimonos or fashionable colorful dresses to weddings, avoiding white (for the bride) or solid black (for funerals).

While it may be easy to follow others at a wedding, the customs at a funeral are more complicated and will depend upon whether it is Buddhist or Shintō. Ask someone about the rituals ahead of time to avoid feeling awkward when you are there.

36
Return Culture Shock

If you have an extended stay in Japan, it may surprise you to find that it is more difficult to readapt to your own culture than it was to living in Japan. For one, when living in a foreign country, local people expect that you will have foreign ideas and foreign customs. They don't expect you to behave exactly like them.

However, you may find people back home are not as understanding. For example, to them, Americans are supposed to think and act like Americans. Any changes they perceive in you are likely to seem alien. Adding to the problem is the way we tend to glorify our own culture when living abroad. ("Back home we would never do things in such a ridiculous manner!") It can be shocking to find that there are just as many inane customs at home. And, what's worse, nobody seems to care or be interested in changing, even if you now know a better way.

People returning to the West after many years in Japan are often surprised at how rude people here seem. They don't go out of their way to show respect to others, especially the elderly, or look out for other people's feelings. People may seem intolerably aggressive to you and the intensity of everything (loud colors, big gestures, pushy advertising) may startle you. You may find that you have a slightly different value system and no shared recent history with others around you. Staying informed on what is going on in your home country while you are away will help ease the transition.

As fascinating as your experiences were, don't expect anyone to have more than a cursory interest. People everywhere tend to be most concerned with their own world, no matter how small that is.

You will have grown and changed as a result of your overseas stay, and it may be frustrating to find that people at home haven't changed much at all. You may need to accept that your time overseas affected you to the degree that some of your old relationships no longer work. People you once enjoyed spending time with may now seem intolerably parochial or unsophisticated. (In the long run, however, you'll probably be happier if you resist the temptation to inform them of this.)

Expect a complete readjustment to take time. The longer you have been away, the longer readapting will take, and it may happen in stages with frustrating plateaus. You may at times feel like you're going crazy—that nothing seems to jibe. One common sign of culture shock is the feeling of being an observer, as though you're watching a movie; you go through the motions but feel distant and uninvolved. Some say the time it takes to completely readjust is similar to the length of time you were gone. Some research indicates that the more visits you make to your home country during your foreign stay, the easier your homecoming will be.

If you ventured abroad as a family unit, your readaptation will probably be easier than for an individual, as you will have people around you with similar experiences and feelings who can provide support through the transition. Take advantage of that by sharing what you are going through. If you are single, try to find a circle of friends who have spent time abroad, or other such support groups. It is important that you have outlets to express your various emotions during this period. Also, try to describe, as much as possible, what you are going through to people who care about you so they can understand your behavior, which may range from being withdrawn to intolerant.

It is important to become reinvolved in your new environment. Read local newspapers and see local movies to have things in common with people around you. It is also good to reserve some regular "alone time" to process the many things you are going through.

Keep track of friends in Japan, even if you're sick of everything Japanese. Before you leave, take lots of pictures of your Japanese friends and acquaintances. Organize them in an album with names, dates, and location. You may become immensely interested in them at a time when your memory doesn't serve you as well as you'd like.

Try to convince your superiors to take advantage of your experience and new expertise. Your company can use this, but it may not have a system set up to do so. You may have to help them understand how you can be utilized and why it is to their advantage. This will serve you well, too, as it will help to give meaning to your experience in Japan in a way that applies to life back home.

Reconciling two very different worlds is not easy. However, in the end it will make your life seem exceptionally rich, and you should eventually be able to apply your experiences in ways that make life more meaningful, not only to you but to those around you.

VII

GENERAL INFORMATION

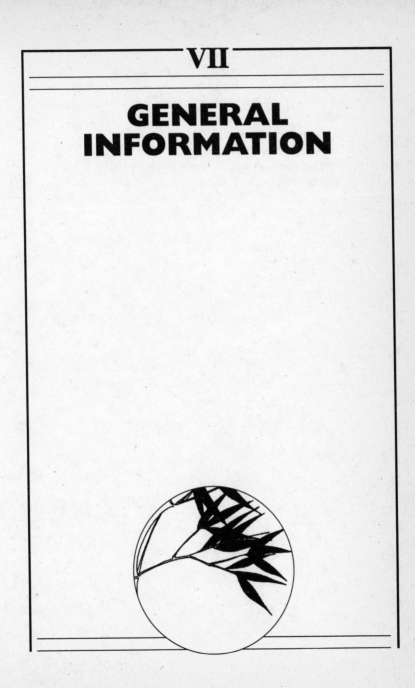

37
Facts on Japan

Geography

Japan is made up of four large islands and about 4,000 small islands, with an aggregate size slightly smaller than California. The largest of the islands is Honshū, containing the capital, Tokyo, and the major cities Yokohama, Osaka, Nagoya, and Kyoto. Honshū is followed in size by the northernmost island, Hokkaidō, the southernmost Kyūshū, and the smallest, Shikoku. Four-fifths of Japan is unarable, mountainous land.

Population

The current population of Japan is 124 million. The populations of major cities, as of March 1990, are as follows:

Greater Tokyo Area	11,631,900
Tokyo	8,006,000
Yokohama	3,211,000
Osaka	2,512,000
Nagoya	2,098,000
Sapporo	1,663,000
Kobe	1,448,000
Kyoto	1,401,000

Fukuoka	1,193,000
Kawasaki	1,153,000
Hiroshima	1,062,000
Kitakyushu	1,020,000

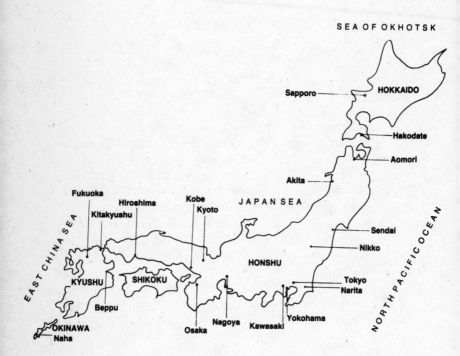

Climate

Tokyo temperatures range from 32° to 50° Fahrenheit (0° to 10° Celsius) in the winter and 86° to 95° Fahrenheit (30° to 35° Celsius) in the summer. The southern islands tend to be warmer all year round. Kyoto is colder than Tokyo in the winter and more hot and humid in summer. The rainy season throughout Japan is mid-June to mid-July. Tokyo gets snow a couple of times a year, but northern Honshū and Hokkaidō generally have snow October through March.

Religion

Although the Japanese are not often thought by Westerners or themselves to be religious, in fact the religion of Japan is woven into the fabric of Japanese life itself. It is a mixture of Shintoism, Buddhism, and Confucianism. The three have been made to fit compatibly together, and each is thought to play its own role in various aspects of Japanese life. None of these religions involves going regularly to a place of worship, but many families have both Buddhist and Shintō altars in their homes at which respect is paid regularly.

Shintoism is the name given to the indigenous native worship of Japan to distinguish it from Buddhism. In the past, all living things, inanimate objects, and natural phenomena were thought to have a spiritual essence that was revered. Harmony and the inseparability of man and nature were a strong part of Shintō beliefs.

Every clan had its own guardian deity, usually thought to have been an ancestor. The clan from which the emperor is descended worshiped the sun goddess; as the power of this clan increased, so did the importance of the sun goddess.

The places of Shintō worship are called shrines (*jinja*) and can be distinguished by the archways (often red, wooden ones) in front of them.

Buddhism was brought to Japan in the sixth century A.D. It teaches nonviolence and respect for all living things (*geta*, the Japanese wooden clogs, were a result of the Buddhist ban on killing animals). Shintō concerns itself with life and living things, while Buddhism addresses death and the afterlife. Funerals are still overwhelmingly Buddhist affairs.

Zen, which literally translates as "silent meditation," was brought from China around the thirteenth century. Zen concentrates on discipline and austerity, teaching one to look for the Buddha within and to live this fleeting life with dignity and calm.

Buddhist places of worship are called temples (*o-tera*) and usually have names that end in *ji* (another reading of the character for "temple").

More a philosophy than a religion, *Confucianism* places strong importance on duty, filial piety, and loyalty to superiors. The five basic relationships that must be properly maintained are lord/subject, father/son, husband/wife, older brother/younger brother, and friend/friend. Because the first four relationships are considered to be vertical, rather than equal, there is still a strong hierarchical social system in Japan today.

Christianity began in Japan with the arrival of Francis Xavier and two other Jesuit missionaries in 1549. For a variety of reasons, Catholicism was well received and spread from the Jesuits' port of landing in Kyūshū throughout southern Japan. By the early 1600s, Catholicism claimed more than 200,000 converts.

Struggle for political power between Christian sects and the desire by the shogunate to preserve political autonomy led to the banishment of foreign missionaries and to persecution of converts. Many Christians died and many reverted to indigenous religions, but at least four thousand Christians and their descendants went underground for 225 years until a Roman Catholic church was constructed in Nagasaki in 1865.

Today in Japan there are about 930,000 Christians who constitute less than 1 percent of the population. There are a number of Christian universities, of which the best known are Sophia and the International Christian University in Tokyo and Dōshisha in Kyoto. (To locate a Christian or Jewish place of worship, see appendix B.) In keeping with the Japanese attitude about honoring all religions, some Japanese Christians celebrate Buddhist holidays and adhere to Shintō ideas.

Religion and Business

While religion does not directly affect business practices in Japan, purification or prayers for the prosperity of an enterprise may be performed by a Shintō priest. A religious ritual frequently accompanies a ground breaking or the opening of a new office. Failure to perform such a ritual when opening a factory in Japan may lead to hiring difficulties. A Shintō altar (a *kamidana*) may be seen in the office of a company president.

38
Travel and Telephone Hints

In your travel to Japan it is important to hit the ground running. Your time will probably be limited as it is so expensive to stay there. This will be difficult if you're experiencing jet lag. However, if you take the proper steps you can minimize the effects.

Managing Jet Lag

While on the plane avoid drinking alcohol and caffeine, both of which accelerate dehydration. Try to drink lots of water during your flight. Eat only when you are hungry, and take your own snacks with you.

Once you arrive, eat lightly; a carbohydrate dinner will help you sleep. Try to get some exercise to get rid of a lactic acid buildup that will make you feel sluggish. Go to bed as close to "normal" local bedtime as possible to minimize feeling tired the next day.

Avoid scheduling heavy business on the first day to give yourself time to get adjusted and focused. Especially if you are alone, build in a break during the week. If you are part of a group traveling together, debrief as a team. Talk to others in your group about how you are feeling. Remember that cycles of culture shock are normal.

In addition, take relaxation materials (tapes, books, etc.) with you to help you unwind.

Travel to Japan

After you clear Customs at Narita Airport, there are a variety of ways to get to downtown Tokyo. The newest and fastest way is via Narita Express, which takes about an hour to an hour and a half, depending on your destination. It makes stops at Tokyo Station, Yokohama, Ikebukuro, and Shinjuku. The cost is about ¥3,000 ($23 at ¥130 = $1). The Airport Express or Limousine Bus stops at the major hotels downtown and costs ¥2,600–2,900 (about $20). Another option is to take the Airport Limousine bus to Tokyo City Airport Terminal (TCAT) at Hakozaki Station at ¥2,700 ($21). You may go by shuttle bus and Keisei Railways Skyliner (to Ueno Station) for ¥1750 ($13). Horror stories about the price of a cab to downtown Tokyo from Narita are true. It will cost you about ¥24,000 ($184). Be aware that the airport is very busy on Sundays. You will probably have to take your luggage up and down flights of stairs on the way to your hotel from the airport, so pack accordingly. You may send your luggage from the airport to your destination via a delivery service costing about ¥2,000 ($15) per piece if under 30 kilos (66 pounds). See the information booth at the airport for details. Your baggage may arrive at your hotel the following day, so don't send anything you will immediately need.

If you are flying into Osaka International Airport, there is limousine bus service to Kyoto Station (¥830, about $6.40), to Shin-Osaka (¥320, about $2.50), and to Osaka Station (¥410, about $3). Taxi service to central Kyoto is about ¥12,000 ($92), ¥4,500 ($34) to downtown Osaka and ¥10,000 ($77) to downtown Kobe.

A ¥2,000 (about $15) passenger service facility charge will be required at check-in for all adults leaving from Narita Airport, Tokyo.

Immigration

Americans can stay in Japan for ninety days without a visa. If you will be working or studying in Japan for an extended period, you will need to obtain a visa from a Japanese consulate prior to your departure. See appendix E for Japanese consulates located in the

United States and Canada as well as Japanese immigration offices. If you plan to stay longer than ninety days at one time, you must apply for alien registration at your city or ward office in Japan. Bring your passport and three five-by-five-centimeter photographs. Passports must be carried with you at all times until you obtain an alien registration card; then the registration card must be carried.

Dealing with immigration may take time. Go early, when the crowds are small. If you work for a prominent Japanese company and fear you will have problems, a phone call ahead of time from the right person can make a difference.

The most convenient immigration office for travelers is in the Tokyo City Air Terminal (TCAT) at Hakozaki on the second floor, but refer to appendix E for addresses of immigration offices throughout Japan.

Controlled Substances

Narcotics are highly controlled substances, carrying severe fines and jail sentences. Marijuana is not at all socially accepted and is viewed as a narcotic. It would be wise to confine your indulgences to alcohol during your stay in Japan.

As some prescription and over-the-counter medications are prohibited, you should check with an embassy or consulate before you attempt to take any in with you.

Also forbidden are books and pictures considered detrimental to public security or morals. This includes magazine pictures that display pubic hair.

Domestic Air Travel

There are three major domestic Japanese airlines: Japan Air Lines, All Nippon Airways, and Japan Air Systems. You may purchase tickets at a travel agency or at an airport. JAL has tickets available in vending machines for the Tokyo–Osaka flights.

Reservations may be made by calling the airlines directly as well as through an agency. JTB (Japan Travel Bureau or Kōtsū Kōsha) is very useful for all tickets. Offices can be found in nearly every train station area. International return flights should be reconfirmed seventy-two hours before departure.

Railways

The *shinkansen,* popularly referred to as the bullet train, has the well-earned reputation of being the fastest and most punctual in the world. A train leaves Tokyo every fifteen minutes.

The *shinkansen* will take you from Tokyo to Kyoto in three hours, from Tokyo to Kobe in three and a half hours, and from Tokyo to Beppu in eight and an half, including a change in trains. Going north from Tokyo, it is about two hours to Sendai and sixteen hours to Sapporo. The new Nozomi *shinkansen* gets from Tokyo to Osaka in two and a half hours. With the Nozomi you can leave Tokyo at 6:00 A.M. and arrive in Osaka on time for a 9:00 meeting.

Reserved seats and express trains (such as the *shinkansen*) cost extra. First class is called the Green Car. Tickets may be purchased at special windows displaying a green clover leaf.

The *shinkansen* is not equipped to handle much luggage. Up to two pieces may be carried on and stored in the overhead racks. Three additional pieces weighing up to 198 pounds (90 kilograms) may be checked. Announcements of departures are made three to five minutes beforehand. Stops are very brief—only about one to two minutes—so be ready to exit with all your luggage as soon as the train stops.

Most *shinkansen* have a dining car as well as a stand-up buffet car for coffee, drinks, and snacks. Vendors also come through the aisles regularly selling box lunches (*bento*), coffee, tangerines, and snacks.

If you are flying JAL, they will make *shinkansen* arrangements for you from the United States or Canada. Otherwise, you will have to make reservations through an authorized travel agent.

Shinkansen tickets can be purchased at almost any large station in Tokyo. Travel Service Centers (*Ryokō Sentā,*) which have someone available who speaks English, are open from 9:00 A.M. to 6:00 P.M., Monday through Friday. You can find them also at many of the large stations. Again, JTB is also very useful.

For a view of Mount Fuji on your way west, sit on the right side of the train (C or D seat). Mount Fuji will come into view about forty-five minutes out of Tokyo.

Japan Rail Passes for seven, fourteen, and twenty-one days are available through travel agents, but *these passes must be purchased outside Japan.*

Information on fares and timetables for all Japanese public transportation can be obtained from the Japan National Tourist Organization, Japan Travel Bureau Offices, and Tourist Information Centers (see appendix C for locations).

When traveling during the long holidays (from the end of December through the first week of January, from the end of April to the beginning of May, July and around the middle of August), be sure to reserve well in advance. Note that many cars are smoking cars. If you want a nonsmoking car, inquire ahead of time.

Porters can be found only at major stations; they charge a set fee.

Subways and Buses

Subways (*chikatetsu*) are an efficient way of getting around most large cities in Japan. To buy your ticket, first find your destination and the appropriate fare on the subway map near the ticket machines. Deposit your money in one of the machines and push the button that corresponds to your fare. Take your ticket and any change. Many Japanese commute into cities by commuter trains run by Japan Railways or other private railways such as Odakyū, Keiō, or Seibu in Tokyo. Try to avoid subways during rush hour—trains are packed beyond capacity! The sardine effect may literally lift you off your feet until you reach your destination. The subways run from roughly 5:00 A.M. to midnight.

Buses are convenient and usually frequent in cities. In Tokyo, you usually need to enter through the front door and pay the fare immediately. Otherwise, enter through the side door and pull a ticket that has a number on it. An electronic sign at the front of the bus displays the numbers and corresponding fares. As you leave the bus, check the fare displayed on the electronic signboard and deposit that amount in the cash box next to the driver.

Taxis

When taking a taxi from an airport or train station, you will find two lines for two sizes of taxis and, of course, two prices. The larger and more expensive taxis usually have the shorter line. Queue up in front of the sign of the taxi size you want. When your turn arrives, don't attempt to open the car door yourself. The driver will do this for you by means of a lever by his seat. The lever also opens the door for you when you're getting out. Warning: Standing back saves shins.

Many taxis have miniature television sets for your enjoyment.

Whenever you're taking a taxi, if your destination is other than a popularly known or public place, it is *imperative* that you have directions written in detail, in Japanese, on a piece of paper that you can hand to the driver. It is virtually impossible to find a residence by mere address. Not only are buildings not numbered consecutively, but dozens of places have the same address. Always carry a card or matchbook from your hotel.

Every mile or so there will be a small police booth (*kōban*), with a couple of policemen who can help point you in the right direction.

Taxis are reasonable, but there is a substantial additional fee for the hours between 11:00 P.M. and 5:00 A.M. Getting a taxi between 11:00 and 11:30 P.M. can be extremely difficult, as this is when the nightclubs close. Do not expect the driver to have change for anything larger than a ¥1,000 bill. Many cabs have automatically printed receipts. These are useful for accounting purposes and for locating forgotten belongings later.

Avoid rush hours on all surface transportation: 7:30–9:00 A.M. and 5:00–6:30 P.M. Allow much more time to travel across Tokyo by taxi, at any time, than you would in most other cities in the world.

Telephones

You can call anywhere in Japan on any public phone. The phones come in different colors and have different capacities:

Red phones take ten-yen coins, up to six at a time.
Blue phones take ten-yen coins, up to ten at a time.
Yellow phones take ten-yen coins, up to ten, and hundred-yen coins, up to nine.
Green phones take ten-yen and hundred-yen coins, and telephone credit cards.

Telephone credit cards are magnetic prepaid cards that can be bought almost everywhere, including department stores, convenience shops, telephone offices, and through vending machines. A convenient feature of the cards is that they register how many "call units" are left on the card. Telephone cards can only be used on green and gray phones. International calls may be placed on gray phones or on green phones with a gold front. Some new green phones and the new gray phones, which are a high-tech version of the green phones, have a digital display panel for instructions and digital and analog jacks for plugging in communications equipment such as modems and fax machines.

A dial tone will be audible only after you insert a coin. Ten yen will buy slightly less than a three-minute local call or shorter long-distance call. A faint warning sound means you are out of time and must quickly insert another coin (or coins, for long distance). To be sure you don't get cut off, add plenty of coins; the warning tone is hard to hear. Any coins not required for your call will be returned to you.

It is almost impossible to locate a person by looking them up in the phone book. Therefore, always have the business card of a client or contact handy if you wish to give them a call.

Nippon Telegraph and Telephone (NTT) recently changed Tokyo telephone numbers from seven to eight digits. If you have an old number that looks like this: 03-502-1461, you must add an extra 3 as the first digit of the main part of the number to make it 03-3502-1461.

Travel and other information is available in English on blue, yellow, or private phones. (Refer to appendix B for a listing of such useful numbers.)

Some visitors find it convenient to rent or lease a telephone pager. Since it gives a digital readout of the number of the person calling you, it makes it easy for people to reach you if you are on the go all day. You simply call them back at the nearest phone. The price is very reasonable compared with a regular telephone. Contact NTT for details. Cellular phone prices are also coming down and can even be rented by the day from new businesses specializing in this service.

39
A Japanese Datebook

This chapter is provided to help you take advantage of some of Japan's rich traditions and also to help you to avoid times when businesses might be closed or travel difficult.

The two periods to avoid are Golden Week (April 29 through May 5) and *o-bon* week. During Golden Week, the Japanese flock to every tourist spot in the country and every form of transportation is packed. *O-bon* is tricky because in some areas it's mid-July and in others it's mid-August, but it's the time when people return to their hometown to honor their ancestors. As in the West, New Year's is a time when people are inaccessible.

National Holidays

(When a holiday falls on a Sunday, it is observed on a Monday.)

January 1 through 3: New Year's celebrations (some places close until the 6th)
January 15: Adults' Day
February 11: National Foundation Day
March 20 or 21: Vernal Equinox Day
April 29: Green Day (formerly Emperor Hirohito's birthday)
May 3: Constitution Memorial Day
May 5: Children's Day

September 15: Respect for the Aged Day
September 23 or 24: Autumnal Equinox Day
October 10: Health-Sports Day
November 3: Culture Day
November 23: Labor Thanksgiving Day
December 23: Emperor's Birthday

Festivals and Celebrations

The Japanese love festivals, and one is observed every day of the year somewhere in the country. The following traditional holidays are observed nationwide and with an enthusiasm seen only at Christmastime in the West.

January 1 through 3: O-shōgatsu is a time for dressing in one's best kimono.

People visit temples, shrines, friends, and relatives, greeting all with, *"Shinnen akemashite, o-medetō gozaimasu"* (Congratulations on the opening of the New Year). Do not wish someone "Happy New Year" before the fact, as Westerners might toward the end of December. This phrase is to be said on or after January 1. An informal New Year's meeting is held on the first day back at work. Great effort is made to start the new year on a positive note.

February 3 or 4: Setsubun, the bean-throwing ceremony. At homes, shrines, and temples, people fervently throw beans at invisible "devils" and recite, "Out with the devil, in with good fortune!"

March 3: Girls' Day. Elaborate and very expensive sets of dolls are displayed in homes and public places.

March 20 or 21: Higan. The Vernal Equinox is a time when people visit ancestral graves. It celebrates the coming of spring.

April 29: Green Day is the start of Golden Week.

May 1: May Day is a time for peaceful protests by socialists, communists, and labor unions.

May 5: Children's Day used to be Boy's Day. Carp-shaped streamers are hung from bamboo poles. (Carp symbolize strength.)

July 7: Tanabata Star Festival. This honors the time when the Weaver Girl on one side of the Milky Way is permitted to meet with her lover, the Shepherd Boy, on the other side. Poems and wishes are written on colored slips of paper and tied to bamboo.

July 15 or August 15: O-bon. The celebration in honor of dead ancestors. The exact date depends on the moon and the locality. People return to their hometowns and set out lanterns to light the way back for their ancestors. Bonfires in the shape of certain characters are lit on the hills around Kyoto. Around *o-bon* is also the mid-year gift-giving season, *o-chūgen*.

September 23: Autumnal Equinox. Again, a time to honor one's ancestors.

October 10: Sports Day commemorates the 1964 Olympics in Tokyo.

November 3: Culture Day, previously the Meiji Emperor's birthday.

November 15: Seven-Five-Three or (*Shichi-go-san*) festival, for girls aged seven and three and boys of five and three. Parents dress the children in new and expensive attire, then take them to shrines and thank the gods for their survival through the early years.

December: Bonenkai (end of year) parties are held in offices and with one's friends to "forget the old year." Christmas celebrations are often incorporated into it. Presents called *o-seibo* are given. Businesses also use this time to reflect on the year's mistakes and plan for a prosperous new year.

December 31: New Year's Eve, *ōmisoka,* is to be spent with the family. At midnight, temples ring their bells 108 times, one time for each of man's earthly desires. Purity is of utmost importance; therefore, people usually do a year-end cleaning in anticipation of the new year but do not clean on New Year's Day, in order to avoid driving good spirits away.

Note that other special occasions may have different emotional connotations from what we would expect. For example, graduation ceremonies, even from primary school, are a time for tears of sadness that people will be parting their ways. This is why the parents (mothers mostly) wear somber clothing.

Counting the Years by Eras

As you can see above, the Japanese follow the Western calendar when they celebrate New Year's Day on January 1. However, rather than using the Christian calendar, the Japanese mark their years by the era of the reigning emperor. For example, the *Showa* era began in 1926 when Crown Prince Hirohito became emperor and ended with his death in 1989. That year was the first of the Heisei era, in which Emperor Akihito reigns. Instead of 1992, for example, the year is known as *Heisei* 4.

Business Cycle

Dates that end with a five or zero such as the fifth, tenth, fifteenth, twentieth, and so on, are used to mark the end of a business cycle. Consequently, these are the busiest days of the month, when bills are paid and deliveries made. The business fiscal year begins April first.

The Chinese Zodiac

The Chinese zodiac, which the Japanese adopted, associates each year with one of twelve corresponding animals. It is believed that those born under a particular sign of the zodiac have distinct personality traits and that certain signs are compatible with each other. The twelve animals (*jūnishi*) are as follows: Rat, Cow, Tiger, Hare, Dragon, Snake, Horse, Sheep, Monkey, Cock, Dog, and Wild Boar. In addition to the animal associated with each year, one of six elements also corresponds to that year, making also a sixty-year zodiacal cycle.

Observances of Western Holidays

The Japanese have "borrowed" many customs and ideas from other countries and have subsequently modified these to suit their own taste and culture. Holidays are no exception. To the Westerner, the Japanese modifications are interesting and give a new perspective to customs we rarely question.

Chocolate companies have promoted Mother's Day and Valentine's Day as a time to give and receive sweets. In Japan, however, on Valentine's Day it is the female who gives chocolate to the men of her choice. It is often thought of as the only day when a woman can assert herself and overtly indicate her interest in someone of the opposite sex. The custom is not limited to sweethearts—in fact, many office ladies feel compelled to give *giri choko* (obligation chocolates) to their superiors at work.

White Day follows on March 14. Men who received chocolate on Valentine's Day indicate interest in the woman by giving her something white, which is usually a marshmallow-based candy. If a man is not interested, he does not give a return gift.

Mother's Day has been celebrated for only a short period of time and is similar to the West's version. Sons and daughters usually give their mothers a red carnation. Stores are also beginning to promote Father's Day as a time to give thanks to Dad with a tie or other small gift.

Halloween is gaining popularity among younger people. However, store displays of Halloween candy are limited to larger cities.

Christmas in Japan is celebrated in a manner very different from in the West. It is not a work holiday but has romantic connotations, with most lovers spending dinner at a fancy restaurant and the night in a luxurious hotel. Most of the popular hotels are booked for Christmas Eve a year in advance. The pressure to find a date to spend the holiday with is great and is a concern of many young people. Many women will make Christmas cakes for their boyfriends and share them on Christmas Eve.

At home, families will also eat Christmas cake after a dinner of fast-food fried chicken. Kentucky Fried Chicken claims that sales on Christmas Eve are five times the average, and many customers order the chicken in advance. It is thought that this alternative to turkey, which is not often eaten in Japan, and the resemblance of Colonel Sanders to Santa Claus are the reasons for Kentucky Fried Chicken's popularity on Christmas Eve.

Birthdays do not have the sense of celebration that they do in the West. While birthday parties are becoming more common, they are not widespread. Today a person's age is usually marked by the passing of a birthday as in the West. However, in the traditional practice, everyone is a year old when they are born, and on New Year's Day everyone becomes a year older. If a baby is born on December 31, 1991, he is two years old on January 1, 1992.

APPENDICES

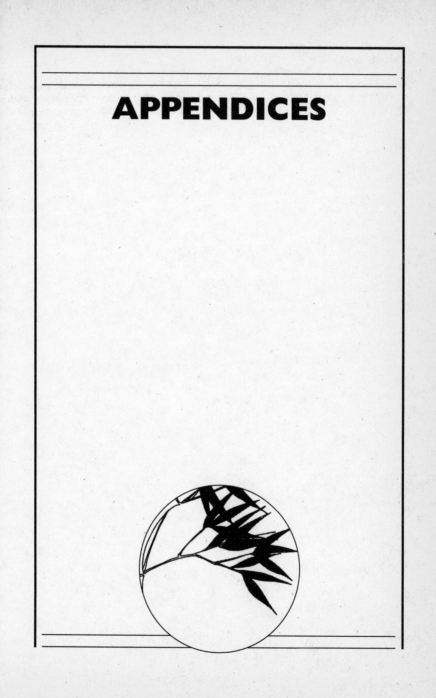

Appendix A
Printers of Japanese Business Cards

Having your business cards printed in Japanese is one indication of your interest and commitment in doing business with the Japanese. In addition to the following list of printers, many airlines provide this service for their customers. Also, some of the major hotels in Japan provide, for a fee, overnight card printing. For a more professional job, though, contact one of the following printers in your area.

To make sure you are able to present your cards with the Japanese right side up, have the Japanese printed horizontally with the top of the Japanese side of the card being the same as the English version on the reverse side.

Los Angeles:

Japan Graphics
202 South San Pedro Street
Los Angeles, CA 90012
213-687-3454

Zero Graphics
424 Boyd Street
Los Angeles, CA 90013
213-680-0253

San Francisco:

KK Graphics
1485 Bayshore Boulevard
San Francisco, CA 94124
415-468-1057

China Cultural Printing Co.
918 Clay Street
San Francisco, CA 94108
415-956-1240

Seattle:

Japan Pacific Publications, Inc.
P.O. Box 3092
Seattle, WA 98114
206-622-7443

West Coast Printing, Inc.
622 Rainier Avenue S.
Seattle, WA 98144
206-323-0441

Chicago:

Japanese Arts & Communication
P.O. Box 11203
612 N. Michigan Avenue
Chicago, IL 60611
312-664-3984

Boston:

Japanese Language Service
186 Lincoln Street
Boston, MA 02111
617-338-2211
1-800-USA-JAPAN
(outside 617 area code)
Also provide translation and
   interpreting services. Research
   using Japanese data bases.

New York:

Hikari Japanese Typesetting
481 Eighth Avenue
New York, NY 10001
212-947-1659

Japan Printing Services
17 John Street
New York, NY 10038
212-406-2905

Gamma Business Form, Inc.
Mr. Nishino
17 John Street
New York, NY 10038
212-997-0400

Canada:

Japan Advertising
1095 W. Pender Street, Suite 1215
Vancouver, B.C. V6E-2M6
604-688-0303

Japan Graphics
669 Denman Street
Vancouver, B.C. V6G-2L3
604-688-7636

Appendix B
Survival Numbers

Emergencies

Police in English (Tokyo)	3581-4321
Police (in Japanese)	110
Fire & Ambulance (in Japanese)	119

General Information

Directory Assistance	104
Directory Assistance (outside the area code)	105
NTT Information Service in English (Tokyo)	3201-1010
in Narita	(0476) 28-1010
in Yokohama	(045) 322-1010

The phone numbers listed below are for Tokyo, unless otherwise indicated. For numbers not listed here, consult the Yellow Pages in the English Telephone Directory available in bookstores or at your hotel.

The Tokyo area code is 03. When calling within Tokyo, it is unnecessary to use this prefix.

Japan Helpline (toll-free help and information 24 hours a day)	0120-46-1997
Time information	117
Weather information	177
Bullet train (to call a passenger)	3248-9311
Travel information (in English)	
Tokyo	3502-1461
Kyoto	(075) 71-5649
When calling outside of these areas for information regarding:	
Eastern Japan (toll free)	0120-222-800

Western Japan (toll free)	0120-444-800
Teletourist taped message	
In English	3503-2911
In French	3503-2926
In Kyoto (in English)	361-2911
Japan Guide Association	3213-2766
American Pharmacy	3271-4034
Lost and found	
Tokyo Metropolitan Police	3814-4151
Japan Railways (JR)	
at Tokyo Station	3231-1880
at Ueno Station	3841-8061
Subways	3834-5577
Buses	3216-2953
Taxis	3355-0300

(If not recovered in three to five days, lost items are usually taken to the metropolitan police.)

International Telephoning Information

In Tokyo	3270-5111
In Osaka	3228-2300
To make a collect call	106
Overseas calls through an operator (in English)	0051

A number of long distance companies offer competitive rates for international calls. For ITJ, use 0041; for IDC, 0061; and for KDD, 001 as access codes. To dial direct overseas, dial in this order: access code, country code, area code, local number.

Counseling and Referrals

Alcoholics Anonymous	3431-8357
Association of Foreign Wives	
(see notices in English-language newspapers)	
International Social Services	3711-5551
Tokyo Community Counseling Services	
(9 A.M. to 12 noon, Monday–Friday)	3434-4992
Tokyo English Lifeline	3264-4347
Human Rights Counseling for Foreigners	3214-6231
Information Corner	
(10 A.M. to 4 P.M., Monday, Wednesday, Friday)	(045) 671-7209
Japan Hotline (10 A.M. to 4 P.M. Monday–Friday)	3586-0110

The Japan Helpline Emergency Service (24 hours)   0120-461-997
Japan Interpreters Association   3209-4741

Judeo-Christian Places of Worship

Tokyo
Baha'i Faith	3209-7521
Christian Science Church	3499-3951
Franciscan Chapel Center	3401-2141
Jewish Community Center	3400-2559
Lutheran Church	3261-3740
Mormon Church	3440-2351
Nicolai Cathedral	3291-1885
Religious Society of Friends	3451-7002
Saint Alban's Church	3431-8534
Saint Ignatius Church	3263-4584
Seventh Day Adventist Church	3401-1171
Tokyo Baptist Church	3461-8425
Tokyo International Church	3464-4512
Tokyo Union Church	3400-0047
Tokyo Unitarian Church	3409-8051

Osaka
Cathedral Church	581-5061
Osaka International Church	768-4385

Useful area codes:
Tokyo 03
Osaka 06
Kyoto 075
Yokohama 045

Appendix C
Helpful Organizations

The JAPAN EXTERNAL TRADE ORGANIZATION (JETRO) is a nonprofit organization set up to promote foreign trade and commerce in Japan. The organization maintains extensive listings of Japanese companies—by commodity—and has available free brochures on just about every aspect of business in Japan. It will set up seminars and offer consultation and evaluation of proposed projects. JETRO also publishes a ten-page newsletter with reports and analyses of Japan's economy, policies, and market opportunities. At regional offices in the United States, a computer database is available that lists information on Japanese importers.

JETRO New York
McGraw-Hill Building, 44th Floor
1221 Avenue of the Americas
New York, NY 10020-1060
212-997-0400

JETRO San Francisco
Quantas Building, Suite 501
360 Post Street
San Francisco, CA 94108
415-392-1333

JETRO Chicago
401 North Michigan Avenue, Suite
  660
Chicago, IL 60611
312-527-9000

JETRO Los Angeles
725 South Figueroa Street, Suite
  1890
Los Angeles, CA 90017
213-624-8855

JETRO Houston
1221 McKinney
One Houston Center, Suite 2360
Houston, TX 77010
713-759-9595

JETRO Atlanta
245 Peachtree Center, Suite 2012
Marquis One Tower
Atlanta, GA 30303
404-681-0600

JETRO Denver
1200 Seventeenth Street, Suite 1110
Denver, CO 80202
303-629-0404

JETRO, Toronto
Britannica House, Suite 700
151 Bloor Street West
Toronto, Ontario, Canada M5S-1T7
416-962-5050

JETRO, Montreal
Place Montreal Trust Tower
Suite 2902
1800 McGill College Avenue
Montreal, Quebec H3A-3J6
514-849-5911

JETRO, Vancouver
World Trade Center, 660
999 Canada Place
Vancouver, B.C., Canada V6C-3E1
604-684-4174

The MANUFACTURED IMPORTS PROMOTION ORGANIZATION (MI-PRO) makes available to interested parties information and catalogs of Western manufacturers with operations in Japan. It also sponsors trade fairs and holds, in Japan, exhibitions that feature foreign commodities.

Manufactured Imports Promotion Organization
Japanese Division
2000 L Street, N.W.
Suite 808
Washington, D.C. 20036
202-659-3729

The EXPORT-IMPORT BANK OF JAPAN is a wholly governmentally owned financial institution working to promote foreign exports to and imports from Japan. It will lend money for joint Japanese–foreign trade ventures.

Export-Import Bank of Japan
2000 Pennsylvania Avenue, N.W.
Suite 3350
Washington, D.C. 20006
202-331-8547

Export-Import Bank of Japan
4–1 Otemachi, 1-chome
Chiyoda-ku, Tokyo 100
03-3287-1221

Export-Import Bank of Japan
Nissei Midosuji Building
Tenth Floor
2–4 Minami-senba, 4-chome
Chuo-ku, Osaka 542
06-241-1771

The JAPAN DEVELOPMENT BANK is a noncommercial, governmentally owned financial institution that will extend loans to Japanese and foreign-affiliated corporations *in Japan*. Loans are for establishing fixed assets, such as factories, and *not* for operations. There is a special loan program for furthering international industrial cooperation in Japan.

601 S. Figueroa St., Suite 4450
Los Angeles, CA 90017-5748
213-362-2980
Fax: 213-362-2982

575 5th Avenue, 28th Floor
New York, NY 10017
212-949-7550
Fax: 212-949-7550

1019-19th St. N.W. Suite 600
Washington, D.C. 20036
202-331-8696
Fax: 202-293-3932

Japan Development Bank
9–1 Otemachi, 1-chome
Chiyoda-ku, Tokyo 100
03-3244-1785/Intl Dept 3-3245-0439

The U.S. DEPARTMENT OF COMMERCE can supply interested parties with details on trade fairs. Persons planning to export to Japan can make use of the department's agency distributor service to help find an agent.

U.S. Department of Commerce
Public Affairs Office
Room 4413
14th Street and Constitution Avenue, N.W.
Washington, D.C. 20230
202-377-4901

The U.S. INTERNATIONAL TRADE COMMISSION has compiled international trade studies, uniform statistical data, and tariff schedules of the United States.

U.S. International Trade Commission
701 E Street, N.W.
Washington, D.C. 20436
202-205-0235

The JAPAN OFFICE OF THE INTERNATIONAL TRADE ADMINISTRATION is an excellent source of information for those who wish to take their product to Japan.

Office of Japan
Room 2318
U.S. Department of Commerce
International Trade Administration
Washington, D.C. 20230
202-377-2425

In Japan, the U.S. EXPORT INFORMATION CENTER (EIC), U.S. & Foreign Commercial Service (US&FCS) of the Embassy of the United States of America, can help establish contacts, provide assistance for conducting business in Japan, and even help negotiate with government officials. At the

Center's library information can be found on Japanese companies. The center also publishes the *Japan Market Information* report and Industry Subsector Analysis reports.

U.S. Export Information Center
U.S. & Foreign Commercial Service
Embassy of the United States of America
10–5, Akasaka 1-chome
Minato-ku, Tokyo 107
03-3224-5075

Information on export services of the U.S. DEPARTMENT OF COMMERCE (USDOC) is also available at 67 district offices throughout the United States and the JAPAN EXPORT INFORMATION CENTER (JEIC) in Washington, D.C. JEIC provides information on doing business in Japan, market entry alternatives, market information and research, product standards and testing requirements, tariffs, and nontariff barriers.

Japan Export Information Center
Room 2318
U.S. Department of Commerce
International Trade Administration
Washington, D.C. 20230
202-377-2425

The FEDERATION OF ECONOMIC ORGANIZATIONS, or *Keidanren,* is Japan's most powerful business organization. It is industry's spokesperson to the Japanese government. It does copious amounts of research on economic issues and will act as a go-between for its various constituent firms.

Federation of Economic Organizations
Keidanren Kaikan
9–4 Otemachi, 1-chome
Chiyoda-ku, Tokyo 100
03-3279-1411

The JAPAN INSTITUTE FOR SOCIAL AND ECONOMIC AFFAIRS, or *Keizai Koho Center,* is a nonprofit organization that works cooperatively with the Federation of Economic Organizations (see above).

Japan Institute for Social and Economic Affairs
Keizai Koho Center
6–1 Otemachi, 1-chome
Chiyoda-ku, Tokyo 100
03-3201-1415

THE JAPAN ECONOMIC INSTITUTE is funded by the Japan Ministry of Foreign Affairs. They write reports on U.S.–Japanese economic relations and foreign policy. You can subscribe to a weekly report on these matters or a monthly business report on joint ventures and mergers.

The Japan Economic Institute
Suite 211
1000 Connecticut Avenue, N.W.
Washington, D.C. 20036
202-296-5633

Important governmental resources in Japan include the following:

THE MINISTRY OF INTERNATIONAL TRADE AND INDUSTRY (MITI) has recently been making efforts to increase imports into Japan by offering incentives to Japanese companies who do so. MITI even has people in the United States who are on the lookout for potential imports from small and medium-sized American companies.

Ministry of International Trade and Industry
Overseas Public Affairs Office
1–3–1 Kasumigaseki
Chiyoda-ku, Tokyo 100
03-3501-1654
Fax: 03-3501-2081

Ministry of Foreign Affairs
Public Information and Cultural Affairs Bureau
2–2–1 Kasumigaseki
Chiyoda-ku, Tokyo 100
03-3580-3311

The AMERICAN CHAMBER OF COMMERCE OF JAPAN can be one of the most useful organizations to join for persons planning to establish operations in Japan. The Chamber researches various critical aspects of commerce in Japan for American businesses: patents and trademarks, employment practices, taxation, financial services, small-business expansion, investments, and trade expansion. Members of the Chamber receive its monthly *Journal* in addition to a newsletter, books, and manuals. The Chamber also sponsors programs and seminars of current interest. This is a good place to network.

American Chamber of Commerce in Japan
Seventh Floor
Fukide Building #2
1–21 Toranomon, 4-chome
Minato-ku, Tokyo 105
03-3433-5381
Fax: 03-3436-1446

JAPANESE BANKS are a good source of information as well as contacts with wholesalers and retailers. They have available information regarding competition, new technology, interested parties and their credit ratings, the Japanese marketplace, and legal issues.

GENERAL TRADING COMPANIES (*sōgō-shōsha*), besides facilitating the flow of imports and exports throughout the world, are involved in commerce at many other levels. They can provide information such as market conditions as well as supply contacts, distribution channels, and access to their great intelligence-gathering arm. They act as *shōkai-sha, chūkai-sha,* freight forwarders, financiers, coordinators, and organizers, and they are frequently involved in joint ventures.

If one is dealing with a relatively small volume, SPECIALIZED TRADING COMPANIES *(senmon shōsha)* might be the better way to go. The companies can provide a more personalized service than the enormous general trading companies.

Many of the MAJOR HOTELS in Japan have BUSINESS INFORMATION SERVICE CENTERS that may be particularly helpful for foreign business people. Here, one can arrange for interpreters, secretarial assistance, and equipment rental.

The JAPAN NATIONAL TOURIST ORGANIZATION (JNTO), a governmental organization created to promote tourism to Japan, has available brochures, books, films, and general materials on Japan in their offices around the world, as well as in almost any city in Japan.

JNTO United States
  Suite 2101
  630 Fifth Avenue
  New York, NY 10111
  212-757-5640

  Suite 601
  360 Post Street
  San Francisco, CA 94108
  415-989-7140

  Suite 770
  410 North Michigan Avenue
  Chicago, IL 60611
  312-222-0874

  Suite 980
  2121 San Jacinto Street
  LB-53
  Dallas, TX 75201
  214-741-4931

Suite 1611
1 Wilshire Building
624 South Grand Avenue
Los Angeles, CA 90017
213-623-1952

JNTO Canada
165 University Avenue
Toronto, Ontario, M5H-3B8
416-366-7140

JNTO has Tourist Information Centers (TIC) in Japan. Their services range from travel information and recommendations to arranging for home visits. They do not, however, handle reservations.

6–6, Yurakucho 1-chome
Chiyoda-ku, Tokyo
03-3502-1461

Airport Terminal Building
Narita, Chiba Pref.
0476-32-8711

Kyoto Tower Building
Higashi-Shiokojicho
Shimogyo-ku, Kyoto
075-371-5649

The JAPAN TRAVEL BUREAU (JTB) is Japan's largest travel agency. In addition to travel assistance throughout Japan, it will provide resource material on Japanese culture and history as produced by the Bureau's huge publishing division.

Japan Travel Bureau International
11th Floor
Equitable Tower
787 Seventh Avenue
New York, NY 10019
212-698-4919

Japanese Travel Bureau
Citicorp Center, 26th Floor
One Sansome Street
San Francisco, CA 94104
415-986-4764

Japan Travel Bureau
Suite 3800
First Interstate Tower
707 Wilshire Boulevard
Los Angeles, CA 90017
213-623-5629

International Travel Division
Japan Travel Bureau
1–13–1 Nihonbashi
Chuo-ku, Tokyo Japan 103
03-3276-7777

Japanese Travel Bureau
Columbia Center, Suite 190
5600 North River Road
Rosemont, IL 60018
708-698-9090

JAPAN AMERICA SOCIETY events in your city are a good way to informally meet people who may be able to provide you with valuable contacts and introductions.

For the Society nearest you, contact:

The National Association of Japan-America Societies
333 East 47th Street
New York, NY 10017
212-715-1218
Fax: 212-755-6752

Your local JAPANESE CHAMBER OF COMMERCE can also be a good source of information and contacts.

If you would like to set up a TEMPORARY OFFICE in the Tokyo area, contact one of the following:

Jardine Business Center in Tokyo
03-3239-2811

Tokyo Executive Center in the
Akasaka area of Tokyo
03-3239-8800

Regus IEO in the Shinjuku area of
Tokyo
03-5379-1331

Japan Business Center near
Makuhari Messe in Chiba
prefecture
0472-97-3131

Relocating to Japan

There are a number of companies in Japan who will assist you in your relocation. A wide variety of services are available, from help in opening a bank account to walking you through your neighborhood.

A service provided to new residents of Tokyo is the Welcome Furoshiki which can be reached at 03-3352-0765, from 9 A.M. to noon, Monday through Friday.

You can buy just about anything from back home through the Foreign Buyer's Club Catalog.

The Foreign Buyer's Club
4–20–5 Yamamoto dori
Chuo-ku, Kobe 650
078-221-2591
Fax: 078-222-3206

The KAISHA SOCIETY is a professional association whose membership consists mostly of foreigners employed at Japanese corporations and academic instiutions. They discuss a wide variety of issues, and bring in guest speakers at their monthly meetings.

Kaisha Society
c/o Research Institute of Industrial
   Relations
Ginza Todoroki Building, 7F
8-16-5 Ginza, Chuo-ku, Tokyo 104

Foreign Executive Women
(Non-Japanese working women)
Jackie Vosburgh
Oji home, Apt. 501
4-22-1 Minami Aoyama
Minato-ku, Tokyo 107
Fax: 03-3403-7516

The TOKYO AMERICAN CLUB is a home away from home for many American expatriates. This club provides a number of amenities for its members, including meeting rooms, full-service restaurants, a library, and gymnasium and pool. You may wish to take guests there. For mid- to upper-middle management Japanese, it is still prestigious to be invited to a function there.

Tokyo American Club
1–2, Azabudai, 2-chome
Minato-ku, Tokyo 104
03-3583-8381
Fax: 03-3583-2888

Support Groups

Foreign Resident's Advisory Center
Tokyo Metropolitan Government
3–8–1 Marunouchi, Chiyoda-ku
(Monday & Thursday 1–4 P.M.)
03-3211-4433

Foreign Residents' Information
   Desk
Meguro Ward Office, Meguro-ku
Chuo-cho 2-4-5
(Monday & Thursday 10 A.M.–noon,
   1–3 P.M.)
03-3715-1111 (ask for *kokusai-ka*,
   International Section)

Human Rights Counseling Center
Tokyo Legal Affairs Bureau
Civil Liberties Department
Otemachi Common Governments
   Office
1–3–3 Otemachi, Chiyoda-ku
(Tuesday & Thursday 1:30–4 P.M.)
03-3214-6231

Other Useful Resources

The AMERICAN CENTER LIBRARIES have English language books but usually do not lend to foreigners.

ABC Kaikan Bldg., 11th Floor
6–3 Shiba Koen 2-chome
Minato-ku, Tokyo 105
03-436-0904

11-5 Nishi Tenma 2-chome
Kita-ku, Osaka 530
06-315-5970

Nagoya Kokusai Center Bldg.
6th Floor
47–1 Nagono 1-chome
Nakamura-ku, Nagoya 450
052-581-8631

Chiyoda Seimei Kyoto Oike Bldg.
9th Floor
Oike-dori Takakura Nishi-iru
Nakagyo-ku, Kyoto 604
075-241-1211

3–36 Tenjin 1-chome
Chuo-ku, Fukuoka 810
092-761-6661

Nishi 28-chome, Odori
Chuo-ku, Sapporo 064
011-641-0211

Japanese consulates in the U.S. and American consulates in Japan are often great sources of information. For their addresses and phone numbers, see appendix E.

Interpreters

The Japan Guide Association
Nihon Kanko Tsūyaku Kyokai
Shin-Kokusai Building #917
3–4–1 Marunouchi
Tokyo
03-3213-2706

Simul International, Inc.
Kowa Bldg. No. 9
1–8–10 Akasaka
Minato-ku
03-3586-8911

CONSULTANTS provide a wide variety of services, from assisting in the development of a particular strategy to introducing potential partners. The Japan Foundation publishes the *Directory of Japanese Specialists and Japan Studies Institutions in the U.S.A. and Canada*, which may be useful. (Available from the Association for Asian Studies in Ann Arbor, Michigan.)

For foreign-managed Japanese advertising services, and negotiation assistance in marketing, media, and entertainment fields:

Ventura Associates, Inc.
Daiko Building
4–2–6 Iidabashi
Chiyoda-Ku
Tokyo, Japan
03-3237-0561
Fax: 03-3237-0562

For consulting services in the computer and semiconductor industries for strategic partnerships, including OEM, distribution, and technical support as well as assistance in information gathering, speech, and presentation preparation:

Enhance, Inc.
Suite 1202
928 Wright Avenue
Mountainview, CA 94043
415-964-7875
Fax: 415-964-7974

For Cross-Cultural Orientations, Negotiation Training, Technical Exchange Seminars, and consulting on Japan and various other areas of the world, or for information on the Cross Cultural Adaptability Inventory:

Rowland & Associates
Suite 308
6920 Miramar Road
San Diego, CA 92121
619-578-9994
Fax: 619-578-9993

For business consulting services for firms targeting the Japanese market, including market research, feasibility studies, entry strategies, partner searches, and investment analysis:

International Business Associates
3600 Wade Street
Los Angeles, CA 90066
310-915-1050
Fax: 310-398-0389

Appendix D
American State and City/County Offices in Japan

Your state's office (as well as some city and county offices) in Japan will provide a number of services, including general advice on market conditions and how to approach the Japanese market, as well as listings of potential Japanese importers. They can also set you up with potential partners or customers through meetings, trade shows, and trade missions that link American and Japanese executives. Sometimes these state offices grant money to businesses so they can participate in trade missions. Unless otherwise indicated, the offices are located in Tokyo; telephone numbers begin with the city code 3 when calling from outside Japan (03 when calling outside of Tokyo in Japan).

State Offices

Alabama
Aoki Bldg., 8th fl.
5–32–8 Shiba
Minato-ku, Tokyo 108
5232-3851
Fax: 5232-3850

Alaska
Toranomon Yamakatsu Bldg.
4–1–40 Toranomon
Minato-ku, Tokyo 105
3436-5285
Fax: 3436-5039

Arkansas
No. 9 Kowa Bldg.
1–8–10 Akasaka
Minato-ku, Tokyo 107
3584-7575
Fax: 3505-4120

California
Kowa 35 Bldg., Annex
1–14–15 Akasaka
Minato-ku, Tokyo 107
3583-3140
Fax: 3584-6613

Colorado
Izumikan-sanbancho
3–8 Sanbancho
Chiyoda-ku, Tokyo 102
3288-3670
Fax: 3288-3677

Connecticut
#1309 KB Plaza
6–11–3 Nishi Shinjuku
Shinjuku-ku, Tokyo 160
3342-7070
Fax: 3342-7043

Delaware
King Homes #108
1–8–10 Kamimeguro
Meguro-ku, Tokyo 153
3477-1851
Fax: 3477-2304

Florida
Win House, Suite 505
1–49–11 Toshin-cho
Itatashi-ku, Tokyo 174
3974-6620
Fax: 3974-0144

Georgia
Kojimachi Hiraoka Bldg., 6th fl.
3–1 Kojimachi
Chiyoda-ku, Tokyo 102
3239-5771
Fax: 3239-5773

Hawaii
Hibiya Kokusai Bldg.
2–2–3 Uchisaiwai-cho
Chiyoda-ku, Tokyo 100
3597-7951
Fax: 3597-7950

Idaho
#2 Takachiho Bldg. 2 fl.
1–6–9 Shiba Daimon
Minato-ku, Tokyo 105
3438-0987
Fax: 3438-4432

Illinois
Sun Kitsukawa Bldg.
1–27–14 Hamamatsu-cho
Minato-ku, Tokyo 105
3578-8111
Fax: 3578-8113

Indiana
Kioichi Residence
4–5 Kojimachi
Chiyoda-ku, Tokyo 102
3230-3526
Fax: 3230-3718

Iowa
No. 31 Kowa Bldg.
3–19–1 Shiroganedai
Minato-ku, Tokyo 108
3444-1988
Fax: 3444-6757

Kansas
Shuwa Kioicho TBR Bldg.
5–7 Kojimachi
Chiyoda-ku, Tokyo 102
3239-2844
Fax: 3239-2848

Kentucky
Seikosha Bldg.
3–4–10 Azabudai
Minato-ku, Tokyo 106
3582-2334
Fax: 3588-1298

Maryland
Yurakucho Bldg. #322
1–10–1 Yuraku-cho
Chiyoda-ku, Tokyo 100
3212-0901
Fax: 3213-7260

Massachusetts
New Diamond Bldg.
1–4–4 Kasumigaseki
Chiyoda-ku, Tokyo 100
3506-9001
Fax: 3506-9003

Michigan
#101 Minami Azabu City House
5–11–7 Minami Azabu
Minato-ku, Tokyo 106
5420-0398
Fax: 5420-0395

Minnesota
Totate Int'l Bldg., c/o Honeywell
    4th fl.
2–12–19 Shibuya
Shibuya-ku, Tokyo 150
3409-3200
Fax: 3409-2770
or
4–32–404 Wakamatsu-cho
Nishinomiya-shi, Hyogo-ken 602
0798-73-1710
Fax: 0798-74-0820

Mississippi
Reinanzaka Bldg.
1–14–2 Akasaka
Minato-ku, Tokyo 107
3588-9027
Fax: 3584-7366

Missouri
Shiba Palace Bldg.
2–1–15 Hamamatsu-cho
Minato-ku, Tokyo 105
3435-8290
Fax: 3435-8207

Montana
Manor Roppongi #303
3–3–28 Roppongi
Minato-ku, Tokyo 106
5563-1765
Fax: 5563-1766

North Carolina
Izumi Shiba-Koen Bldg.
1–6–8 Shiba Koen
Minato-ku, Tokyo 105
3435-9301
Fax: 3435-9303

Nevada
IBO Bldg.
6–10 Yotsuya, 4-chome
Shinjuku-ku, Tokyo 106
3226-3840
Fax: 5379-1345

New Jersey
Kokusai Bldg.
3–1–1 Marunouchi
Chiyoda-ku, Tokyo 100
3213-5330
Fax: 3213-5336

New York
Yurakucho Bldg.
1–10–1 Yuraku-cho
Chiyoda-ku, Tokyo 100
3213-4387
Fax: 3216-0578

Ohio
Hirakawacho Bldg.
2–6–1 Hirakawacho
Chiyoda-ku, Tokyo 102
3262-1312
Fax: 3239-6477

Oklahoma
c/o CRC Research Institute
3–6–2 Nihonbashi-Honcho
Chuo-ku, Tokyo 103
3665-9600
Fax: 5695-7880

Oregon
Yurakucho Denki Bldg., No. Tower
1–7–1 Yuraku-cho
Chiyoda-ku, Tokyo 100
3213-3081
Fax: 3211-8498

Pennsylvania
World Trade Center Bldg.
2–4–1 Hamamatsu-cho
Minato-ku, Tokyo 105
3436-5583
Fax: 3432-4512

South Carolina
Toranomon TBL Bldg.
1–19–9 Toranomon
Minato-ku, Tokyo 105
3591-1604
Fax: 3591-0757

Utah
Silver Takadanobaba Bldg.
3–18–11 Takata
Toshima-ku, Tokyo 171
3986-9361
Fax: 3986-9116

Virginia
Fukoku Seimei Bldg. Ste. 1701
2–2–2 Uchisaiwai-cho
Chiyoda-ku, Tokyo 100
3508-2750
Fax: 3508-2759

Washington
ABS Bldg.
2–4–16 Kudan Minami
Chiyoda-ku, Tokyo 102
3221-9707
Fax: 3239-2817

West Virginia
Nisei Sakaemachi Bldg.
3–24–17 Nishiki
Naka-ku, Nagoya 460
052-953-9798
Fax: 052-953-9795

Wisconsin
Landic Akasaka 2nd Bldg.
2–10–9 Akasaka
Minato-ku, Tokyo 107
3589-4700
Fax: 3589-4777

City/County Offices

Houston, Texas
c/o BOT Research Int'l. Ltd.
1–4–2 Marunouchi
Chiyoda-ku, Tokyo 100
3213-2546
Fax: 3215-5408

New York/New Jersey Port
Kokusai Bldg.
3–1–1 Marunouchi
Chiyoda-ku, Tokyo 100
3213-2856
Fax: 3215-0033

Puerto Rico
Shin Tokyo Bldg.
3–3–1 Marunouchi
Chiyoda-ku, Tokyo 100
3213-5206
Fax: 3213-5208

Richmond, Virginia
c/o Pacific Projects Inc., 9th fl.
1–8–2 Toranomon
Minato-ku, Tokyo 105
3502-0402
Fax: 3508-2047

San Bernardino, California
4–5–21–416 Akasaka
Minato-ku, Tokyo 107
3587-2353
Fax: 3586-7928

Appendix E
Immigration

**Embassy of Japan
(in the United States)**
2520 Massachusetts Avenue, N.W.
Washington, D.C. 20008
202-939-6700

**Consulates of Japan
(in the United States)**
Federal Reserve Plaza
14th Floor
600 Atlantic Avenue
Boston, MA 02210
617-973-9772 or 973-9774

299 Park Avenue, 18th fl.
New York, NY 10171
212-371-8222

100 Colony Square Building
Suite 2000
1175 Peachtree Street, N.E.
Atlanta, GA 30361
404-892-2700

One Poydras Plaza
Suite 2050
639 Loyola Avenue
New Orleans, LA 70113
504-529-2101

Olympia Center
Suite 1000
737 North Michigan Avenue
Chicago, IL 60611
312-280-0400

2519 Commerce Tower
911 Main Street
Kansas City, MO 64105-2076
816-471-0111 or 471-0113

First Interstate Bank Plaza
Suite 5300
1000 Louisiana Street
Houston, TX 77002
713-652-2977

250 East First Street
Suite 1507
Los Angeles, CA 90012
213-624-8305

50 Fremont Street
Suite 2200
San Francisco, CA 94105
415-777-3533

2400 First Interstate Bank Tower
1300 S.W. 5th Avenue
Portland, OR 97201
503-221-1811

601 Union Street
Suite 500
Seattle, WA 98101
206-682-9107

550 West 7th Avenue
Suite 701
Anchorage, AK 99501-3559
907-279-8428

1742 Nuuanu Avenue
Honolulu, HI 96817
808-536-2226

Guam International Trade
Building
Suite 604
590 South Marine Drive
Tamuning, GU 96911

**Embassy of Japan
(in Canada)**
255 Sussex Drive
Ottawa, Ontario K1N-9E6
613-236-8541

**Consulates of Japan
(in Canada)**
Suite 1785
600 Rue de La Gauchetiere
Ouest
Montreal, Quebec H3B-4L8
514-866-3429

2480 ManuLife Place
10180-101 Street
Edmonton, Alberta T5J-3S4
403-422-3752

730-215 Garry Street
Winnipeg, Manitoba R3C-3P3
204-943-5554

900-1177 West Hasting Street
Vancouver, B.C. V6E-2K9
604-684-5868

Suite 2702
Toronto Dominion Bank Tower
P.O. Box 10
Toronto Dominion Centre
Toronto, Ontario M5K-1A1
416-363-7038

Japanese Immigration Offices
1-3-1 Otemachi
Chiyoda-ku, Tokyo
03-213-8111

12-4 Nishi Odori
Chuo-ku, Sapporo
011-261-9211

3-20 Gorin 1-chome
Miyagino-ku, Sendai
0222-56-6076

Narita Airport
0476-32-6812

37-9 Yamashita-cho
Naka-ku, Yokohama
045-681-6801

4-3-1 Sannomaru
Naka-ku, Nagoya
052-951-2391

72-2 Nambu-machi
Fushimi-ku
075-612-0660

2-1-17 Tanimachi
Higashi-ku, Osaka
06-941-0771

Kaigan-dori
Chuo-ku, Kobe
078-391-6377

6-30 Kamihatchobori
Naka-ku, Hiroshima
082-221-4412

1-22 Okihama-cho
Hakata-ku, Fukuoka
092-281-7431

18-2-40 Izumi-cho
Kagoshima
0992-22-5658

1-15-15 Hikawa
Naha, Okinawa
0988-32-9836

Embassy of the United States
1-10-5 Akasaka
Minato-ku, Tokyo
03-3224-5000

**Consulates of the United States
in Japan**
2-11-5 Nishi-tenma
Kita-ku, Osaka 530
06-315-5900

2-5-26 Ōhori
Chuo-ku, Fukuoka
092-751-9331

1 Kita, 28 Nishi
Chuo-ku, Sapporo 064
011-641-1115

2129 Gusukuma
Urasoe-shi, Naha, Okinawa
0988-77-8142

Appendix F
Recommended Reading

General

Choate, Pat. *Agents of Influence*. New York: Knopf, 1990.

Christopher, Robert. *The Japanese Mind: The Goliath Explained*. New York: Simon & Schuster, 1983.

Dore, Ronald. *Taking Japan Seriously: A Confucian Perspective on Leading Economic Issues*. Stanford: Stanford University Press, 1987.

Kawasaki, Ichiro. *Japan Unmasked*. Rutland, VT: Tuttle, 1969.

Ohmae, Kenichi. *Fact and Friction*. Tokyo: Japan Times, 1990.

———. *The Borderless World: Power and Strategy in the Interlinked Economy*. New York: Harper Business, 1990.

Powell, Jim. *The Gnomes of Tokyo: The Positive Impact of Foreign Investment in North America*. New York: American Management Associate, 1989.

Prestowitz, Clyde V. *Trading Places: How We Are Giving Our Future to Japan and How to Reclaim it*. New York: Basic Books, 1989.

Reischauer, Edwin O. *The Japanese Today*. Cambridge, MA: Harvard University Press, 1988.

Business

Abegglen, James C., and George Stalk, Jr. *Kaisha: The Japanese Corporation*. New York: Basic Books, 1985.

Clark, Rodney. *The Japanese Company*. Tokyo: Charles Tuttle, 1979.

Deutsch, Mitchell. *Doing Business with the Japanese*. New York: New American Library, 1983.

Fallows, James. *More Like Us: Putting America's Native Strengths and Tradi-*

tional Values to Work to Overcome the Asian Challenge. Boston: Houghton Mifflin, 1989.

Huddleston, Jackson N. *Gaijin Kaisha: Running a Foreign Business in Japan*. New York: M.E. Sharpe, 1990.

JETRO. *Doing Business in Japan*. Tokyo: Gakuseisha Publishing, 1984.

Kang, T. W. *Gaishi: The Foreign Company in Japan*. New York: Basic Books.

Kato, Hiroki, and Joan Kato. *Understanding and Working with the Japanese Business World*. New Jersey: Prentice Hall, 1992.

Kester, Carl. *Japanese Takeovers: The Global Contest for Corporate Control*. Cambridge, Mass.: M.I.T. Press, 1990.

Ohmae, Kenichi. *Mind of the Strategist: The Art of Japanese Business*. New York: McGraw Hill, 1982.

Prindle, Tamae K., translator and editor. *Made in Japan and Other Japanese "Business Novels."* New York: M.E. Sharpe, 1989.

"Salaryman" in Japan. Tokyo: Japan Travel Bureau, 1986.

Tatsuno, Sheridan. *Created in Japan: From Imitators to World-Class Innovators*. New York: Harper & Row, 1990.

Thian, Helene. *Setting Up and Operating a Business in Japan: A Handbook for Foreign Businessmen*. Tokyo: Tuttle, 1988.

Yoshino, M. Y., and Thomas B. Lifson. *The Invisible Link: Japan's Sogo Shosha and the Organization of Trade*. Cambridge, Mass.: The MIT Press, 1986.

Zimmerman, Mark. *How to Do Business with the Japanese: A Strategy for Success*. New York: Random House, 1985.

Negotiating

Graham, John L., and Yoshihiro Sano. *Smart Bargaining: Doing Business with the Japanese*. Cambridge, Mass.: Ballinger Publishing, 1984.

March, Robert M. *The Japanese Negotiator: Subtlety and Strategy Beyond Western Logic*. Tokyo: Kodansha, 1988.

Moran, Robert T. *Getting Your Yen's Worth: How to Negotiate with Japan, Inc.* Texas: Gulf Publishing Company, 1985.

Musashi, Miyamoto. *A Book of Five Rings: The Classic Guide to Strategy*. New York: Overlook Press, 1974.

Cultural

Benedict, Ruth. *The Chrysanthemum and the Sword*. Boston: Houghton Mifflin, 1946.

Condon, John C. *With Respect to the Japanese: A Guide for Americans.* Washington: Intercultural Press, 1984.

Doi, Takeo. *The Anatomy of Dependence.* Tokyo: Kodansha, 1971.

———. *The Anatomy of Self.* Tokyo: Kodansha, 1990.

Keene, Donald. *Appreciations of Japanese Culture.* Tokyo, New York, San Francisco: Kodansha, 1981.

Libra, Takie Sugiyama. *Japanese Patterns of Behavior.* Honolulu: University Press of Hawaii, 1976.

Morton, W. Scott. *Japan: Its History and Culture.* New York: McGraw-Hill, 1984.

Nakane, Chie. *Japanese Society.* Berkeley: University of California Press, 1970.

Okakura, Kakuzo. *The Book of Tea.* New York: Dover, 1964.

Smith, Robert J. *Japanese Society: Traditions, Self and the Social Order.* New York: Cambridge University Press, 1983.

Suzuki, Shunryu. *Zen Mind, Beginner's Mind.* New York and Tokyo: John Weatherhill, 1970.

Van Wolfern, Karel. *The Enigma of Japanese Power.* New York: Knopf, 1989.

Whiting, Robert. *You Gotta Have Wa.* New York: Random House, 1989.

Language

Akuyama, Nobu, and Carol Akuyama. *Talking Business in Japanese.* New York: Barron's, 1988.

Association for Japanese Language Teaching. *Japanese for Busy People I & II.* Tokyo, New York, San Francisco: Kodansha, 1984.

Association for Overseas Technical Scholarship. *The AOTS Japanese-English Dictionary for Technical Study.* Tokyo: 3A Corporation.

Cleary, Thomas. *The Japanese Art of War: Understanding the Culture and Strategy.* Boston: Shambala, 1992.

Editions Berlitz. *Japanese for Travellers.* Lausanne, Switzerland: Berlitz, 1984.

Hall, Edward T., and Mildred Reed Hall. *Hidden Differences: Doing Business with the Japanese.* New York: Doubleday, 1987.

Inter-Cultural Institute of Japan. *Survival Japanese—The ABCs of Japanese.* Tokyo: The Inter-Cultural Institute of Japan.

Jorden, Eleanor Harz. *Beginning Japanese—Parts 1 and 2.* New Haven and London: Yale University Press, 1963. Tapes also available.

Kodansha International. *Kodansha's Compact Kanji Guide.* Tokyo: Kodansha International.

Matsumoto, Michiro. *The Unspoken Way—Haragei: Silence in Japanese Business and Society.* Tokyo: Kodansha, 1988.

Mitsubishi Corporation. *Tatemae and Honne: Distinguishing Between Good Form and Real Intention in Japanese Business Culture.* New York: The Free Press, 1988.

Mizutani, Osamu. *Japanese: The Spoken Language in Japanese Life*. Tokyo: The Japan Times, 1982.

Mizutani, Osamu, and Nobuko Mizutani. *Nihongo Notes*. Tokyo: The Japan Times, 1977.

Nagara, Susumu. *Japanese for Everyone*. Tokyo: Kodansha.

Nissan Motor Company, Ltd. *Business Japanese*. Tokyo: Passport Books, 1984.

Niyekawa, Agnes. *Minimum Essential Politeness: A Guide to Japanese Honorific Language*. New York: Kodansha, 1991.

Sadler, A. L. *Code of the Samurai: The Spirit that Drives Japan*. Vermont: Tuttle, 1941.

Travel/Living in Japan

Ashby, Janet. *Gaijin's Guide: Practical Help for Everyday Life in Japan*. Tokyo: The Japan Times, 1985.

Baedeker's Tokyo: The Complete Illustrated City Guide. Great Britain: Jarrold & Sons Ltd, 1983.

The Economist Business Traveler's Guide to Japan. New York: Prentice Hall Press, 1987.

Ekiguchi, Kunio. *Gift Wrapping: Creative Ideas From Japan*. Tokyo: Kodansha, 1985.

Kanno, Eiji, and Constance O'Keefe. *Japan Solo*. New York: Warner Books, 1988.

Kinoshita, June, and Nicholas Palevsky. *Gateway to Japan*. Tokyo: Kondansha, 1990.

Popham, Peter. *The Insider's Guide to Japan*. Hunter Publishing, 1987.

Shibusawa, Tazuko, and Joy Norton. *The Japan Experience: Coping and Beyond*. Tokyo: The Japan Times, 1989.

Wolf, Reinhart. *Japan: The Beauty of Food*. Rizzoli Publishing, 1987.

Reference Books

Diamond's Japan Business Directory. Diamond Lead Company, 4–2 Kasumigaseki, 1-Chome, Chiyoda-ku, Tokyo, Japan.

Diamond's Who's Who in Japanese Business. Diamond Lead Company, 4–2 Kasumigaseki, 1-Chome, Chiyoda-ku, Tokyo, Japan.

Directory of Information Sources in Japan. Japan Special Libraries Association, Kinokuniya Book Store Co., Ltd., 17–1 Shinjuku-ku, Tokyo 160–91.

Economic World: Directory of Japanese Companies in the USA. Economic Salon Ltd., 60 East 42nd Street, New York, NY 10165.

Industrial Groupings in Japan. Published biannually by Dodwell Marketing

Consultants, C.P.O. Box 297, Tokyo, Japan. Tel: 03-3589-0207, Fax: 03-3589-0516.

Japan Company Handbook. Tokyo: Tokyo Keizai Shinposha. Biannual.

Japan Economic Almanac. Tokyo: Nihon Keizai Shinbun.

Japan Update. Published quarterly by Keizai Koho Center, Tokyo, Japan.

Japan 199—: An International Comparison. Tokyo: Keizai Koho Center. Annual.

Standard Trade Index of Japan. Tokyo: The Japan Chamber of Commerce and Industry.

Two Japanese "Who's Who" volumes (*Jinji Koshinroku* and *Zen Nippon Shinshiroku*) are packed with valuable information in Japanese. These books are available for reference at many banks, the Chamber of Commerce, Japanese Consulates, and JETRO.

For a good selection of books on Japan: Kinokuniya Book Stores in New York, San Francisco, San Jose, Los Angeles, Seattle.

For a six part video series, *Working with Japan,* contact ITRI at 800-626-2047.

For other videos dealing with living abroad and the multi-cultural workforce contact Copeland Griggs Productions at 415-668-4200.

Appendix G
Periodicals

Asian Wall Street Journal Weekly. World Financial Center, 200 Liberty Street, New York, New York, 10281. 1-800-628-9320.

Business Japan. Nihon Kogyo Shimbun, Suite 518, 41 East 42nd Street, New York, New York 10017. Also Sankei Building, 7–2 Otemachi, 1-chome, Chiyoda-ku, Tokyo 100.

The East. 19–7–101 Minami-Azabu 3, Minato-ku, Tokyo.

The Economic Eye. Keizai Koho Center, Otemachi Building, 6–1 Otemachi, 1-chome, Chiyoda-ku, Tokyo 101.

Economic World. Economic Solon, Ltd., 60 East 42nd Street, New York, New York 10165.

Industrial News Weekly. Industrial News Agency, 3–10 Kanda Ogawa-cho, Chiyoda-ku, Tokyo 101.

Japan Automotive News. Automotive Herald Company, Ltd., Shinto Building #3, 5–21–5 Shinbashi, Minato-ku, Tokyo 105.

Japan Commerce and Industry. The Japan Chamber of Commerce and Industry, Suite 505, World Trade Center Building, 4–1 Hamamatsu-cho, Minato-ku, Tokyo, 105.

The Japan Industrial & Technological Bulletin. Japan External Trade Organization, Machinery and Technology Department, 2–5 Toranomon, 2-chome, Minato-ku, Tokyo 105.

Japan Petroleum & Energy Weekly. Japan Petroleum Consultants, Ltd., Sanwa Building #3, 4-5-4 Lidabashi, Chiyoda-ku, Tokyo 102.

Japan Publications Guide. Intercontinental Marketing Corporation, IPO Box 5056, Tokyo 100-31.

The Japan Quarterly. Asahi Shimbun, 5–3–2 Tsukiji, Chuo-ku, Tokyo 104.

Japan Steel Journal. Japan Iron & Steel Journal Company, Ltd., Ohki-Sudacho Building, Sixth Floor, 1–23 Kanda, Sudacho, Chiyoda-ku, Tokyo 101.

Journal of Japanese Trade & Industry. Japan Trade & Industry Publicity,

Inc., Toranomon Kotohira Kaikan, 2–8 Toranomon, 1-chome, Minato-ku, Tokyo 105.

Nikkei Financial Daily, The Nikkei Industrial Daily, The Nikkei Marketing Journal, and *The Nikkei Weekly.* Nihon Keizai Shimbun, Inc., 1–9–5 Otemachi, Chiyoda-ku, Tokyo 100-66. *New York office:* 1325 Avenue of the Americas, Suite 2500, New York, NY 10019. *Los Angeles office:* Suite 1515, 725 S. Figueroa Street, Los Angeles, California 90017.

Speaking of Japan. Keizai Koho Center, Otemachi Building, 6–1 Otemachi, 1-chome, Chiyoda-ku, Tokyo 100.

Tokyo Journal. Cross-Culture Jigyodan Company, Ltd., 3-F Magatani Building, 5–10–13 Toranomon, Minato-ku, Tokyo 105.

Tokyo Weekender. Oriental Building, 55–11 Yayoi-cho, 1-chome, Nakano-ku, Tokyo 164.

U.S. Japan Business Review. 256 S. Los Angeles St., Los Angeles, California, 90012.

Glossary

ah sō desu ka: "is that so?"

aisatsu: greeting.

akachōchin: literally, red lantern; a pub with a red lantern hanging at its door.

amae: "sweet," indulgent dependence.

amakudari: retired bureaucrat entering private enterprise as senior executive.

anago: eel.

apāto: apartment.

arigatō: "thanks."

arigatō gozaimasu: "thank you very much."

arigatō gozaimashita: "thank you" (for act that has been completed).

basu: bus.

bentō: box lunch.

bīru: beer.

bōnenkai: end of the year celebration.

bu: department.

buchō: department/division manager.

buchō dairi: deputy department manager.

buchō hosa: assistant department manager.

chadai: "tea money"; a gratuity given to the proprietor at an inn.

chikatetsu: subway.

chōsa-bu: business research department.

chotto matte kudasai: "wait a moment, please."

chūkai-sha: mediator.

deguchi: exit.

dō itashimashite: "you're welcome."

dokutā sutoppu: doctor's orders; phrase useful for declining alcohol.

dōmo: "thanks"; or can be used as greeting.

dōmo arigatō gozaimasu: "thank you very much."

dōzo: "please," as in "please come in"; not a request.

dōzo yoroshiku: "please feel kindly disposed toward me."

ebi: shrimp.

eki: station.

fuku buchō: vice department manager.

fuku kaichō: vice chairman.

fuku shachō: vice president.

fusuma: sliding door covered with thick paper.

futon: sleeping mattress.

ganbaru: persist.

ganbatte kudasai: "hang in there"; "do your best."

geisha: hostess trained to entertain and to perform in traditional dance and music.

genkan: vestibule, entrance porch.

geta: wooden clogs.

gijyutsu-bu: engineering department.

ginkō: bank.

giri choko: obligation chocolates.

go chisō sama: "it was a feast"; "thanks for the meal."

(Global) no (Smith) desu: "I am (Smith) of (Global)."

gokurōsama deshita: "thank you for your trouble."

gomen kudasai: "may I come in, please" "excuse me."

gomen nasai: "excuse me"; "I'm sorry" (informal).

hai: "yes."

hai, wakarimasu: "yes, I understand."

hajimemashite: "it's my first time to have the pleasure to meet you."

hanchō: group leader.

hangaeshi: return gift of about half the value of gift received.

haragei: getting a gut-level feeling.

hashigo: bar hopping.

heisei: the current era.

higan: vernal equinox.

higashi guchi: East exit.

hiragana: phonetic alphabet used for particles and verb endings.

hisho-shitsu: secretariat.

hōmu-bu: legal department.

honbu/honsha: headquarters.

honne: essence, true intentions.

hoshōkin: refundable deposit given to the landlord upon renting an apartment.

hoteru: hotel.

ichi ran hyō: cover sheet for memoranda.

ie: house.

iie: "no."

iie, wakarimasen: "no, I don't understand."

irasshaimase: "welcome" (used mostly in stores and restaurants).

iriguchi: entrance.

ishi no ue nimo sannen: "perserverance brings success."

itadakimasu: "I humbly receive"; uttered before starting a meal.

itsumo osewa ni natte orimasu: "I am always in your debt"; "thank you for everything."

ji: suffix denoting Buddhist temple.

jichō: deputy director.

jinja: Shintō shrine.

jinji-bu: personnel department.

jōmu torishimariyaku: managing director.

jūnishi: twelve Chinese zodiac animals.

ka: group, section.

kabushiki kaisha: corporation.

kachō: section leader, section head.

kachō dairi: deputy section head.

kachō hosa: assistant section head.

kaichō: chairman.

kaiseki ryori: traditional meal.

kaishi: paper napkin used for tea ceremony.

kaizen: continuous improvement in the workplace.

kakarichō: supervisor (subsection head).

kakarichō hosa: assistant supervisor (subsection head).

kamidana: Shintō altar

kangaemashō: "let's think about it."

kanji: characters taken from Chinese.

kanpai: "Cheers!"; toast before drinking.

kansayaku: statutory auditor.

kappa-maki: cucumber *sushi* roll.

karaoke: "singing" bar.

karōshi: death from overwork.

katakana: phonetic alphabet used for foreign words.

katsuo bushi: dried bonito.

keiretsu: corporate groupings.

keiri-bu: accounting department.

kenrikin: "key money"; nonrefundable deposit given to landlord upon renting an apartment.

kikaku-shitsu: corporate planning office.

kikoku shijo: children of returnees.

kinien: no smoking.

kissaten: coffee shop.

kita guchi: north exit.

kōbai-bu: purchasing department.

kōhai: junior person.

kōhii: coffee.

kōhō-bu: public relations department.

konbanwa: "good evening."

konnichiwa: "good afternoon."

kotatsu: heating element, formerly of coals, now an electric lamp, under a low table.

kōtsū kōsha: Japan Travel Bureau.

kyuri: cucumber.

maguro: tuna.

makizushi: *sushi* that is rolled in a sheet of seaweed, then sliced.

man: unit of ten thousand.

manshon: expensive apartment or condominium.

medetai: auspicious, felicitous, joyous.

meishi: business card.

minami guchi: south exit.

minshuku: lodging at a private house.

mizu: water.

mizuhiki: cord made of rolled paper, for wrapping gifts.

mizu shōbai: the entertainment industry, literally the "water trade."

mizu-wari: "cut" with water, as in "scotch and water."

moshi moshi: "hello" (telephone).

mōshiwake gozaimasen: one of strongest ways of saying, "I'm sorry."

ne: "isn't it?"; "you know?" (tacked on to end of sentence).

nengajō: cards sent for New Year's greeting.

nigirizushi: seafood on small blocks of rice.

nishi guchi: west exit.

nomiya: neighborhood pub.

noshi: dried abalone, attached to a present.

o-bon: festival in honor of one's dead ancestors.

o-choko: sake cup.

o-chūgen: midsummer festival; and gift-giving time.

odaiji ni: "take good care of yourself"; said to someone who is sick.

ohayō gozaimasu: "good morning" (informal: *ohayo*).

o-kaeshi: a return gift.

oku: one hundred million.

okusan: title used for speaking to or referring to someone's wife.

okyaku-sama wa kami-sama desu: "the customer is God."

o-mimai: get-well gift.

ōmisoka: New Year's Eve.

o-miyage: souvenirs.

onegai shimasu: "please," as in a request.

onna: female.

onsen: hot springs.

on-za-rokku: "on the rocks," as in "scotch on the rocks."

o-saki ni: phrase uttered when doing anything before someone else.

o-seibo: year-end festival.

osewa ni narimasu: "thank you for your assistance"; phrase used when tipping.

o-shibori: small damp towel given before a meal.

o-shinko maki: sushi made of pickled vegetable.

o-shōgatsu: New Years (January 1–3).

o-te arai: rest room.

otoko: male.

o-toshi-dama: New Year's monetary gift.

o-tsukai-mono: "something you can use"; gift accompanying request for a favor.

otsukaresama deshita: "thank you for your hard work"; said to someone who has worked overtime.

oyasuminasai: "good night."

rabu hoteru: "love hotel."

reikin: "thank-you money"; nonrefundable deposit given to landlord upon renting an apartment.

rikutsuppoi: too logical, too rational, argumentative.

ringi: decision by group; shared authority.

ringi-seido: request for group decision.

ringi-sho: written proposal that is circulated first among peers, then upward for senior approval.

ryokan: traditional Japanese inn.

ryokō sentā: travel service centers.

saah: "hmmm."

sakazuki: sake cup.

-san: suffix denoting respect, attached to a person's family name; equivalent to "Mr." or "Ms."

sashimi: sliced raw fish.

satō san ni yoroshiku: "please give my regards to Mr. Sato."

sayonara: "good-bye."

seisankanri-bu: production control department.

sekihan: white rice with red beans.

sempai: senior person.

senjitsu wa dōmo arigatō gozaimashita: "thank you" (for something that occured recently).

senmon shōsha: specialized trading companies.

senmu torishimariyaku: senior executive managing director.

sensei: title used for speaking to a teacher, doctor, or lawyer.

setsubun: bean-throwing ceremony.

shachō: president.

shain: employee.

shichi-go-san: children's festival for three-, five-, and seven-year-olds.

shikikin: refundable deposit given to the landlord upon renting an apartment.

shinjinrui: "new breed," the younger generation.

shinkansen: "bullet train."
shinnen akemashite o-medetō gozaimasu: "Happy New Year."
shitenchō: branch manager.
shitsu: office.
shochū-mimai: cards sent during mid-summer.
shōhin kaihatsu-shitsu: product development office.
shōji: sliding door covered with rice paper.
shōkai-sha: introducer.
shokuchō: foreman.
shōsha: trading company.
shugi bukuro: envelope for a money gift.
shunin: project head.
soba: buckwheat noodles.
sōdanyaku: senior advisor.
sōgō-shōsha: large general trading company.
sōmen: fine noodles.
sōmu-bu: general affairs department.
sōpurando: "soapland," euphemism for Turkish bathhouse (see *toruko*).
sumimasen: "excuse me."
sunakku: snack shop.
sushi: fish (often raw) served on small blocks of flavored rice.
tai: red snapper.
takushii: taxi.
tamago: egg.
tanabata: Star Festival.
tatami: rice straw mat.
tatemae: form, external appearance.
teishoku: full meal, as opposed to à la carte.
tera: Buddhist temple.
tokonoma: alcove in a *tatami*-mat room.
torishimariyaku: director.
torishimariyaku kai: board of directors.
toruko: Turkish bath, now called *sōpurando*.
tsurekomi hoteru: "love hotel."
udon: wheat noodles.
ūron cha: oolong tea.
unagi: eel.
wakarimasen: "I don't understand."
wakarimasu: "I understand."
wasabi: green horseradish.
wa-shoku: Japanese food.
yakitori: grilled chicken.
yōkoso: "welcome" (informal).
yōkoso irasshaimashita: "welcome."
yoroshiku onegai shimasu: "I hope for your continued goodwill."

yō-shoku: Western food.
yūbinkyoku: post office.
yukata: cotton robe.
zabuton: cushion in *tatami* room.
zaimu-bu: finance department.
zansho-mimai: cards sent toward the end of summer (August).
zashiki: large *tatami*-mat room.
zen: silent meditation.

Index